KNOT MAGIC

KNOT MAGIC

A Handbook of
POWERFUL SPELLS
using Witches' Ladders and other
MAGICAL KNOTS

SARAH BARTLETT

WELLFLEET
PRESS

Brimming with creative inspiration, how-to projects, and useful
information to enrich your everyday life, Quarto Knows is a favorite
destination for those pursuing their interests and passions. Visit our
site and dig deeper with our books into your area of interest:
Quarto Creates, Quarto Cooks, Quarto Homes, Quarto Lives,
Quarto Drives, Quarto Explores, Quarto Gifts, or Quarto Kids.

Copyright © 2020 Quarto Publishing plc,
an imprint of The Quarto Group

This edition published in 2020 by Wellfleet,
an imprint of The Quarto Group,
142 West 36th Street, 4th Floor,
New York, NY 10018, USA
T (212) 779-4972 F (212) 779-6058
www.QuartoKnows.com

First published in 2019 by New Burlington Press,
an imprint of The Quarto Group
The Old Brewery, 6 Blundell Street
London N7 9BH

Wellfleet titles are also available at discount for retail,
wholesale, promotional, and bulk purchase. For
details, contact the Special Sales Manager by email at
specialsales@quarto.com or by mail at The Quarto Group,
Attn: Special Sales Manager, 100 Cummings Center Suite
265D, Beverly, MA 01915 USA.

10 9 8 7 6 5 4 3 2

ISBN: 978-1-57715-214-9

Library of Congress Control Number: 2019956127

Printed in Singapore

Previously published as *Witches' Ladders and Other
Knot Spells*.

Contents

Introduction

Knot spells have been used for thousands of years to empower and sanction beneficial desires.

Along with special incantations, knot enchantments will seal your intentions and invoke positive success. Many of these knotting spells are based on traditional enchantments, but have been updated to include contemporary ingredients for you, the modern-day spell-caster.

This book also includes witches' ladders, as well as "knot-seeing spells"—magical ways to visualize knots without physically doing them. Yet the result is equally effective.

The act of knotting is a ritual whereby you are literally "tying" part of yourself into a spell along with the other ingredients. It's a way of proving and justifying your belief and faith in the magic you wish to happen.

HISTORY

Ancient Greek and Assyrian texts include a wide range of knotting rituals for binding the desired outcome into the spell. One Assyrian spell instructs how to tie a knot discreetly into your shawl as you recite the name of the solar god, so that when you enter to the king's chamber, he will favor you above all others.

A Greek love spell asks that you weave hemp and red wool, knot it 14 times, and at each knot recite a magic spell. Finally, the cord is tied around your waist to attract a lover or to incite desire. Knotting lapis lazuli-colored cord into the hem of your robe would also ensure princes and royalty would bless you with prosperity.

WITCHES' LADDERS

According to folklore, in late 19th-century England, a witches' ladder was found in an attic in Somerset along with a group of brooms and chairs. Believed to be the venue of a witches' coven, the ladder was made up of a length of twine with birds' feathers inserted along its length. Its purpose still

remains a mystery, but the idea took hold as part of the popular revival of all things supernatural, and witches' ladders became an essential tool in spell-making.

Earlier ladder spells can be found as far back as ancient Egypt, Greece, and Rome. Talismans, amulets, feathers, coins, and personal items were woven into knots to reinforce specific desired outcomes. Egyptian fishermen knotted fish skins into a length of rope to promote favorable weather. When the skins dried out, new fish skins were inserted to invoke beneficial winds.

In ancient Eastern traditions, jade and other precious gemstones were knotted into women's knotted girdles to ensure sexual fertility and marriage.

UNKNOTTING SPELLS

Unknotting charms banish all forms of negativity and help you to move on from the past. Tying and then untying knots in this way was popular in Celtic traditions. This ritual was thought to bind and ensure protection or fulfil a request first, then later, untying the knots would release positive energy around you.

So, whether you want to tie the knot for mutual happiness or free yourself from a knotty problem, this spell book is the key to making magic work for you.

About This Book

This unique collection of spells explores the tradition, history, and modern-day practice of knot magic. With a length of string, ribbon, cord, or anything that can be knotted, you can quickly make magic work for you, whether to enchant new love into your life, change your fortune, or manifest your dreams.

THE SPELLS

There are six spell themes—Love & Romance; Home, Family, & Friends; Career & Lifestyle; Prosperity & Abundance; Protection & Spiritual Healing; and Travel & Adventure. There are knots to enhance and reinforce your spells, as well as traditional rituals such as lighting candles, anointing with oils, and sealing intentions by placing them in containers.

Flashes inform you of the best time to practice your spell to achieve the most desirable results.

You are encouraged to read your incantations out loud. When we repeat a verse, we are empowering our voice with words, and also empowering the words with our voice. Language is the most powerful symbolic magic on Earth, so use it to reinforce all your desires.

This book uses the most essential and simplest of magical ingredients, most of which can be found in your home, online, or in local stores.

Beautiful artwork illustrates the different types of knots needed to enhance your spell.

VISUALIZATION SPELLS

Each of the six chapters contains a special knot-seeing spell whereby, instead of the practical work of tying a knot, you only visualize yourself doing it, while focusing and meditating on the illustrations.

The text guides you through your visualization journey.

You are encouraged to reflect on the artwork to help you get into a Zen state of mind.

KNOT DIRECTORY

Most of the knots are simple and quick to tie, but there will be a few for which you may need to follow instructions. The Knot Directory at the back of the book (see pages 116–125) will help you with this. Although certain knots are recommended for specific spells, if you find any of them too difficult, simply use any knot that you feel is appropriate for the spell.

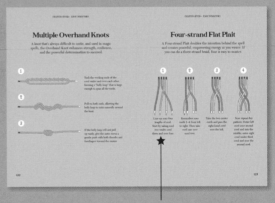

The techniques for tying the different knots are organized into easy-to-follow, step-by-step sequences.

Witches' Oath

Before you start to perform any of the spells in this book, please read the following paragraph and then take the Witches' Oath.

Spells, charms, and enchantments are created by using symbols and ingredients that correspond to our desires or needs. This is, in fact, an ancient practice which, in the words of medieval sorcerers, modern-day Wiccans, and indigenous peoples worldwide, means that "like attracts like" or "as Above, so Below." There is also an old saying that "what goes around comes around, and sometimes tenfold." So, if you put out bad energy or thoughts, then you will eventually find it comes back to bother you too. That's why, when performing knot spells, you are not just creating magic for you alone, you are also doing it for the good of the whole. Never curse another person—you can banish their bad or negative energy from your life, but should never cause them harm. When you think "magic," you're thinking "Universe." That means giving out the best possible vibes to create positive energy and harmony everywhere, including for yourself.

REMEMBER THE WITCHES' OATH:

"I will only do what I do for the good of all."

Magical Association Chart

	DEITIES	PLANET/ZODIAC	ELEMENTS
LOVE	APHRODITE, RATI, BRANWEN	LIBRA, TAURUS, VENUS	EARTH, AIR
HOME, FAMILY, FRIENDS	HESTIA, FRIGG, VISHNU	VIRGO, CANCER, MOON	WATER, EARTH
CAREER, LIFESTYLE	ZEUS, GANESHA, THOR	SUN, SATURN, JUPITER, CAPRICORN	FIRE, AIR, EARTH
PROSPERITY, ABUNDANCE	APOLLO, HELIOS, RA	SUN, PLUTO, URANUS, AQUARIUS	FIRE, AIR, EARTH
PROTECTION, HEALING	HATHOR, SELENE, ISIS	MOON, CANCER, NEPTUNE, PISCES	WATER, EARTH
TRAVEL, ADVENTURE	ZEUS, HERMES, JANUS	MERCURY, JUPITER, MARS, SAGITTARIUS	FIRE, AIR, EARTH

By symbolic association, colors, deities, numbers, astrological symbols, elements, crystals, and planets all interrelate and correspond to one another. Once you start to associate a particular color with a crystal or a plant with a goddess, then you can add ingredients of your own to enhance or reinforce the spell.

NUMBERS	COLORS	CRYSTALS	PLANTS/OILS
2, 3, 5, 7	RED, PINK, WHITE	ROSE QUARTZ, RED CARNELIAN, GARNET	ROSE, JASMINE, PATCHOULI, APPLE, MINT
1, 2, 4, 8	GREEN, BLUE, BLACK	BLACK TOURMALINE, WHITE QUARTZ, MALACHITE	BASIL, ROSEMARY, CINAMMON, TEA TREE
1, 5, 7, 9	YELLOW, GOLD, GREEN	SUNSTONE, CITRINE, AVENTURINE, JADE	SUNFLOWER, SANDALWOOD, OLIVE, CEDAR
2, 4, 9	YELLOW, WHITE, RED	CITRINE, PEARL, TIGER'S EYE	BASIL, RICE, SUNFLOWER
2, 4, 6, 8	BLUE, PURPLE, BLACK	RUBY, BLACK TOURMALINE, ONYX	JASMINE, LAVENDER, GARLIC
1, 5, 7, 9	RED, GREEN, YELLOW, WHITE	SUNSTONE, SHUNGITE, AVENTURINE	CLOVER, GINGER, CITRUS

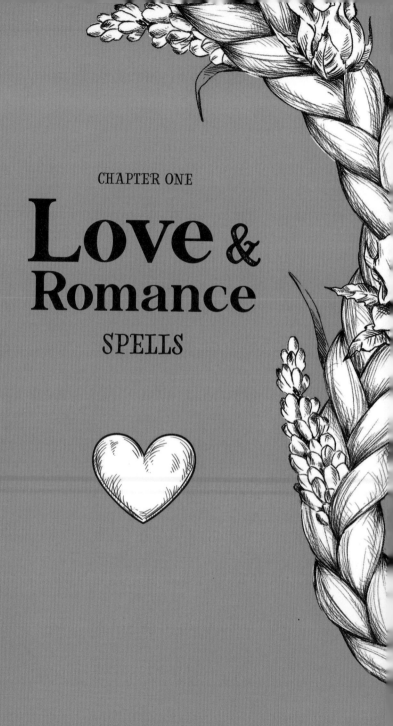

CHAPTER ONE

Love &
Romance

SPELLS

We all look for love in one way or another.
It may be a breathtaking new romance, a commitment
or long-term bond, or just a change in the way we
interact as a couple. In the ancient Greek magic
papyri, over 70 percent of the spells described
were charms to invoke desire, passion, and lust.
Whatever your particular need, these spells will
enable you to spellbind, create harmony in the
bedroom, free yourself from past heartache,
divine your future lover's intention, or ensure
long-term commitment with the one you love.
So, leap in, and enjoy tying a few love knots.

Five-knot Enchantment to Attract Romance

This is an easy way to attract new romance into your life using a secret ribbon charm that was popular with the ladies of medieval courts.

Medieval courtly love was a coded tradition intended to promote chivalry among the nobility, whereby love-lorn knights and courtiers were spellbound by one lady of the court. These seductive she-devils held romantic power over their ardent lover and would toss braided ribbons to their favorite knight as he jousted at tournaments. If he caught the ribbon, it was his right to adore her forever and be her champion. So why not make someone your champion now?

WHAT YOU WILL NEED

Rose quartz crystal (to amplify the power of love)

2 red candles (to symbolize you and another)

Lighter or matches

2 x 3ft (90cm) ribbons (one red and one white)

Rose essential oil

SPELL CASTING

Put your rose quartz crystal on a table with the two candles placed on either side. Light the candles and then take up the two ribbons. Tie the ribbons at one end, then weave them together, crossing one over the other in a simple, two-ribbon braid. As you do this, say the first enchantment (opposite) out loud. When you have finished, knot the ends of the ribbons together.

Continue braiding the ribbons and include three equally spaced knots in the length. Again, repeat the enchantment as you do so.

Next, dribble a little rose oil on each of the five knots and say aloud the second enchantment (opposite).

Finally, place the knotted ribbons in a circle round the crystal. Blow out the candles and leave your knotted petition until after the next Full Moon to attract magical romance your way.

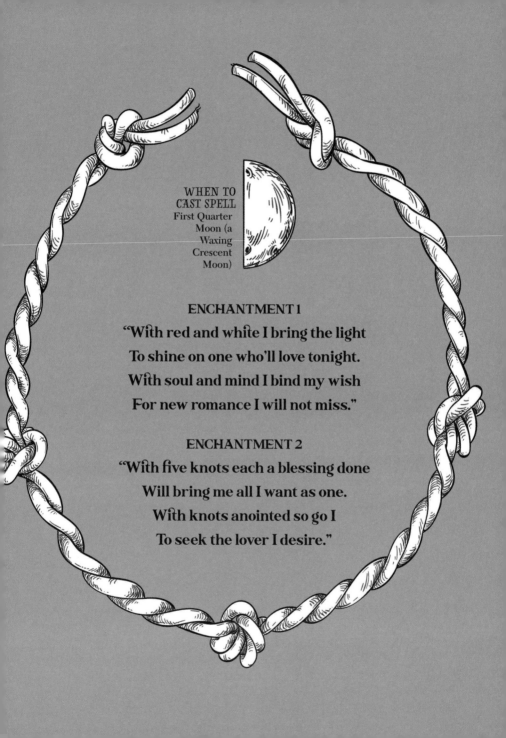

WHEN TO
CAST SPELL
First Quarter
Moon (a
Waxing
Crescent
Moon)

ENCHANTMENT 1
"With red and white I bring the light
To shine on one who'll love tonight.
With soul and mind I bind my wish
For new romance I will not miss."

ENCHANTMENT 2
"With five knots each a blessing done
Will bring me all I want as one.
With knots anointed so go I
To seek the lover I desire."

Aphrodite's Seduction Charm

Sometimes we want more than just teasing texts, and meeting up with that cheeky player can either stir our passions or turn us off. But if physical desire overwhelms us, what of the other? Have they fallen for us, or are they playing hard to get? How can we seduce them into our lives? This braided chain will quickly maximize your seductive powers.

A phrodite was the Greek goddess of love, sexuality, and beauty. This vain deity was more concerned with pleasing herself than pleasing others, yet by petitioning her and drawing on her power, you too can seduce anyone you want into your arms. This braided chain, commonly known as a Monkey Braid, resembles the love net that Aphrodite's blacksmith husband made of gold in order to trap Ares and Aphrodite as they lay together.

You too can "capture" this seductive passion for yourself and let the magic work on someone of your choice.

WHAT YOU WILL NEED

Golden cord (the length is up to you)

Aphrodite's Magic Circle of Doves (as drawn opposite)

SPELL CASTING

Follow the instructions on page 118 to make a chain of Monkey Braid from the golden cord. As you make each loop in the chain, recite the following mantra.

*"I will be with the one I desire
They will be with me by my side."*

When you reach the end of the length of cord, tie off the knot at the working end and coil it around Aphrodite's Magic Circle of Doves. Once the chain is in place, chant the spell (opposite).

After you have recited the spell, bless the chain by kissing it and say the name of your intended lover or date for the magic to work.

"By wings of doves and goddess power
Seductive joy for all the hours
I'll take to greet the lover dear
Who'll kiss my lips and hold me here."

WHEN TO CAST SPELL

Before you
go on a date
or out on a
seductive
hunt

Black Lace Sensual Empowerment Posy

In Middle Eastern traditions, patchouli was used to enhance sexual desire. Used here with the magical benefits of jasmine and lavender essential oils, it creates the perfect sexual-harmony posy.

Black lace is associated with elegance and erotic lingerie. A 17th-century lace-making school in Chantilly, France, became the center for black-lace ruffles, flounces, and trimmings for aristocratic European fashionistas. Sadly, during the French Revolution, most of these lace-makers were guillotined because of their links to Marie-Antoinette. However, by the end of the 19th century, black lace was back in fashion and became identified with elegance, eroticism, and feminine sexuality. So, to bring passion into your love life, create this black-lace lust posy, and enjoy.

WHAT YOU WILL NEED

3 black candles

Lighter or matches

Mirror

2–3ft (60–90 cm) length of black lace trimming

Jasmine essential oil

Patchouli essential oil

8 stems of lavender flowers

SPELL CASTING

Light two of the candles and place them in front of the mirror. With no other light on, gaze into the mirror for a while and focus positive thoughts on your own, or you and your partner's, sexual needs.

Take up the length of black lace and wrap it around the third candle three times, leaving enough at each end to make a knotted bow, repeating the spell chant (opposite) as you do so.

Sprinkle a few drops of the jasmine and patchouli oils onto the lace, then gently push the lavender stems into the knot of the bow to make a posy.

Repeat the spell chant as you do so and then place the candle posy upright in front of the mirror, or lay it down with the wick of the candle pointing toward the mirror.

Blow out the two lit candles, place the posy under your bed, and let the magic begin.

WHEN TO
CAST SPELL
Late at night,
preferably
during a
Waxing
Crescent Moon

"By jasmine, candle, oil, and lace
With flowers of blue and mirrored face
My pleasure comes and so does thine
To bring us both a loving time.
Patchouli sends us sensual bliss
While black lace wraps our lover's kiss
In wildest dreams of fancies thus
And skin to skin we love to lust."

"They Love Me, They Love Me Not" Divining Spell

Divine the truth about whether someone loves you or loves you not with this easy knot enchantment.

D ivination is a way of seeing. It's not so much prediction, more a sense of intuitive understanding about what will happen in the future. This simple spell propels you into your intuitive self, where you really "know" the truth before it happens. Although it's possible for you to cheat with this simple spell, it's rather like tossing a coin and saying, "Heads, I will go to the party," and "Tails, I won't." So, the coin lands tails up, but you know deep inside that you will go to party because deep down you know that this is what you want. It's a way of confirming your own deepest truths.

WHAT YOU WILL NEED

5 strands of gold-colored thread

Magical Eight Divining Circle (as drawn opposite)

A pinch or two of dried basil leaves

SPELL CASTING

Take the five lengths of thread, which should be long enough to make a circle around the Magical Eight Divining Circle. Using any knot you like, tie seven knots throughout the length of the five threads while repeating the following charm:

"This knotted thread brings truth to me, each knot for love, or not to be."

Place the knotted threads around the circle, starting to the East and ending to the Northeast. Sprinkle the basil leaves over the knots and then close your eyes.

Move your fingers slowly over the knots five times from East to Northeast, saying at the first knot, "They love me," then at the next knot, "They love me not," and so on. When you reach the final knot before the Northeast, this will tell you whether they love you or not.

WHEN TO
CAST SPELL
On a sunny day
for clarity and
illumination

Eternally You and I

Creating a Celtic love knot is the key to it manifesting and ensuring permanent love between you and your partner.

The Celtic love knot, a well-known symbol of eternal love between two people, was traditionally exchanged in many pre-nuptial Celtic folk ceremonies as a token of loyalty. The bride and groom exchanged tokens, whether engraved rings, knotted straw, or tied ribbons, then feasted outside at dusk in the wild meadows, dancing and merry-making long into the evening. Rooted in ancient spiritual traditions, the abstract design is also a variation of other decorative knotted motifs representing eternity which appeared in religious and secular decoration.

On the opposite page is a diagram of a Celtic knot that you will need to work with too.

WHAT YOU WILL NEED

Length of white cord (for perfect harmony)

2 rose quartz crystals (for harmonious union)

2 rings, one silver (for lunar energy) and one gold (for solar energy)

SPELL CASTING

Create your Celtic Knot (see page 119), and, while you do so, focus on your lover and all the positive plans for the future you have made together. Place the knot on a window ledge where it can draw down the energy of the Sun and the Moon for one lunar cycle (New Moon to New Moon).

Place the two rose quartz crystals on either side of the love knot, one to the East, one to the West. Place the gold ring to the North of the knot and the silver to the South.

Take up the love knot in the palm of your hand, while you repeat the enchantment (opposite).

Leave your petition to the Universe for a complete lunar cycle to ensure complete harmony between you and your partner.

"This knot of love invokes our truth
Our mutual strength, our union too.
This knot of love invokes the Moon
To bring us joy or dance our tune.
This knot of love invokes the Sun
To tie the knot so two are one."

Untying the Knot
for Letting Go

This visualization technique requires nothing more than a quiet space, a candle to amplify a sense of autonomy, and the page in front of you.

O f course, some relationships end. The ideal romance or love affair can go quite wrong, and we can be left feeling hurt or betrayed, regretful, mourning our loss, or sometimes even glad but guilt-ridden for our share in the story. It can be very hard to get out of this state of blame, self-pity, or "If only" thinking. Yet there is a way. We tie knots to make love work, so when love doesn't work we have to untie those knots, either literally or via the knotted tricks of the mind which keep us bound by our illusions or fears.

Sit in a comfortable place, light a candle, and make sure you won't be disturbed for at least 10 minutes. Gaze at the image of knotted ribbons tied around the railings of a bridge. These are knots left by many lovers to show their loyalty to one another. One of the knots is yours. It doesn't matter how long ago it was that you left it there, you know which is yours and you're going to untie it.

There are hundreds of knots, some faded, others tattered and torn by the elements, and others brand new, silky, and shining in the breeze. Beneath the bridge is a fast-flowing

river, carrying sticks and weeds downstream to the sea.

Imagine yourself walking across this bridge, knowing that your knotted ribbon is there, but, before you get to the other side of the bridge, you must untie the knot and throw it away forever to show that you can let go of the past and not be bound to it any more. Then you can look back without regret, move on, and start again—but only by releasing your ribbon into the river.

As you walk across the bridge, imagine you see your ribbon, which is looking a little worse for wear. Gently bend down and untie it. However hard the knot is to unravel, you know you will do it. Eventually the knot comes away and you have the tattered ribbon in your hand. Now lean over the railing and let it drop down into the rushing stream. Watch the ribbon as it flows fast and disappears beneath the foam on its journey away from you.

Now walk to the other side of the bridge, and know you have crossed this one at last and that one day you may return with a new ribbon, a new knot to tie, and another love.

Commitment Spell— Tying the Knot

When we first date someone, we are never sure if it's going to become a committed and exclusive relationship. We may believe that's what the other person wants, but sometimes we're not in a position to ask, nor even to expect that of them. But if you truly believe this is the lover or partner for you, then this simple spell will help to ensure an exclusive commitment for however long you want that to be.

P re-Christian marriage ceremonies often included the ritual of "hand-fasting," which is still favored by modern witches and pagan followers today. This tradition of binding a length of cloth or ribbon around the bride and groom's hands was used to promote the couple's fidelity and love for one another. A poem or incantation was recited to seal the lover's knot. This spell will ensure you can get the kind of commitment you're looking for.

For this spell you're going to use the well-known Reef Knot, which signifies equality and balance, harmony, and togetherness. Make sure to tie it exactly as described or you might end up with an unbalanced granny knot.

WHAT YOU WILL NEED

A handful of dried or fresh rosebuds

Incense burner or oil diffuser

Incense sticks or essential oils for the diffuser (one each of sandalwood and patchouli)

Lighter or matches

2 x 1ft (30cm) ribbons (one red and one white)

Indelible gold pen

SPELL CASTING

Around dusk (it was traditionally believed that the sun-god, Helios, would ride his chariot across the heavens at dusk and return in the morning with the love ribbons made sacred), gently cast the rosebuds onto a flat surface, indoors or outdoors. Wherever you find a place that feels right, set down your diffuser or incense burner, asking the Universe to bless it by saying:

"This place is forever true."

Place the diffuser or burner in this center and light the stick or oil. Take the red ribbon and tie a Reef Knot (see page 121) with the two ends, so that you have made a reasonably long loop, but with long ends left at the knot. Take the white ribbon

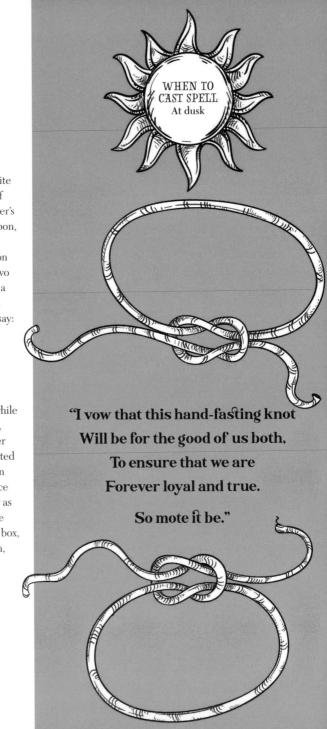

and do the same thing. Next, write your name in gold on the loop of the white ribbon and your partner's name on the loop of the red ribbon, and chant the spell (right).

Finally, attach the white ribbon to the red ribbon by using the two ends of the white ribbon tied in a Reef Knot round the red ribbon loop. Once you have done this, say:

*"We are as one,
two golden loves, red love,
white love, bound this way."*

Focus on the knotted petition while you repeat the charm five times, and then extinguish your diffuser or incense sticks. Place the knotted ribbons and the rosebuds in a tin or small lidded box in a safe place to ensure your love is bound for as long as you wish. If you want the relationship to end, remove the box, scatter the rosebuds in the earth, and untie the knots.

**"I vow that this hand-fasting knot
Will be for the good of us both,
To ensure that we are
Forever loyal and true.**

So mote it be."

Witches' Ladder Love Spell

So, you've fallen in love and are ready for an exclusive relationship. Or perhaps you're already coupled up and want to ensure long-lasting loyalty and trust. This witches' love ladder will bind any long-term love with magical joy.

In most ancient cultures worldwide, hair was braided not only to attract a lover, but also to reveal a woman's marital status. The Greek goddess of love, Aphrodite, was often depicted with elaborately braided tresses, while the seductive witch goddess Circe was described by Homer as having braided locks. Like weaving, braiding your desires weaves true love into your relationship.

Red is associated with passion, pink with romance, and white with loyalty, while roses and lavender are traditional symbols of long-lasting love. The total number of items woven into this braid is six, the numerological magic number of commitment and marriage. So, get cracking and braid your desire for long-term happiness into being.

WHAT YOU WILL NEED

3 wide ribbons (one red, one pink, and one white), each 2–3ft (60–90cm) in length

White candle

Lighter or matches

3 rosebuds (with short stems)

3 sprigs of lavender

SPELL CASTING

Take the three ribbons and knot them together at the top. Light the candle, relax, and visualize all you want from this relationship. Repeat the spell (opposite) as you braid.

After three braids, secure a rosebud on the red ribbon. After another three braids, secure a lavender sprig on the red ribbon. After a further three braids, place the second rosebud on the pink ribbon; then, after three more braids, a lavender sprig on the pink ribbon, then the third rosebud on the white ribbon, and the last lavender sprig on the white ribbon.

Once all items are knotted, seal the witches' ladder by tying a final knot at the end and repeating the complete spell once more, adding:

"The energy of me and you is stored forever here, so mote it be."

Blow out the candle and keep your love ladder in a safe place.

WHEN TO
CAST SPELL
After sunset

"With braids so true
The first rose woos.
With knots so tight
My love's alight.
With braids so fair
The next rose cares.
With lavender flowers
My love's empowered.
With knots divine
The last rose binds
And stores our love
Both mine and thine."

CHAPTER TWO

Home, Family, & Friends

SPELLS

Our home is one of the most sacred places to each of us, in whatever shape or form it is. Our space is ideally one where we can relax, indulge in our private world and individual quirks, or feel comforted by a sense of belonging and security. But not all of us experience this. We may have difficult family members, friends who bother us day and night, or we feel lonely or just that we don't belong to anything or anywhere. This chapter of spells will ensure that you can bring harmony into your home, keep your friends happy, and invoke goodness among family too.

Woven Herb Garland for a Harmonious Home

The most important thing for most of us is to have harmony in the home. After all, this is the place we want to relax, get away from the busy outside world, or entertain our friends and family.

This is a traditional woven garland of knotted herbs and flowers which, when hung in the main entrance, will enhance harmony in your home. It was usually renewed every year around the spring equinox in Celtic and Wiccan traditions. Tea rituals are part of many Eastern traditional family gatherings to welcome and bless guests in the home. Include your own tea ritual to enhance this wellbeing spell for everyone in the family, even if they are not present.

WHAT YOU WILL NEED

Handfuls of basil, rosemary, thyme, and sage stems

A selection of twigs

5 cinnamon sticks

Green tea

Teapot

Cup or mug

3 x 5ft (1.5m) lengths of thick twine, straw, cord, or rope

1ft (30cm) length of green ribbon

SPELL CASTING

Lay out all your ingredients on a table and make the green tea.

Knot the ends of the three lengths together, attaching them to a post or other a solid base, and make a simple three-strand braid. Knot off at the ends. Shape the braid into a circle and tie the ends together with the green ribbon.

Sip some of the tea and then repeat the charm (opposite).

Take up your various herbs, twigs, and cinnamon, and begin to arrange them in your garland, weaving them into the braid until the garland is mostly covered with vegetation.

As you work, keep sipping your tea and repeat the charm at least five times.

Once your garland is complete, attach it to a wall and harmonious living will continue for as long as it is hanging there. Like the ancients, renew every year to stimulate fresh energy and growth in the home.

New Moon or
spring equinox,
or when you move
into a new home

"With this garland woven be
With nature's bounty
Most will see.
How warm this home,
How loved this place
With spirits blessed
And soulful grace."

Friendship Braid

Friendship bracelets are traditionally given to a good friend in order to seal the bond between you. Every knot is a sign of those special bonds. This simple, four-braided bracelet is for yourself and will carry the energy of peace, acceptance, and empathy between you and friends, both old and new.

This charm draws on the four energies of the four archangels of Christian iconography—and also in magical lore—which are associated with the four Winds of Change. These guardian angels are ready to blow delightful experiences into your social life for togetherness and harmony.

In magic, the Four Winds are aligned to the archangels: Uriel—North Wind; Michael—South Wind; Raphael—East Wind; and Gabriel—West Wind.

WHAT YOU WILL NEED

4 fine strands of silk thread or cord (to represent each of the angels) in the following colors, plus four candles in the same colors:

White (East)
Green (North)
Red (South)
Blue (West)

White quartz crystal

Lighter or matches

SPELL CASTING

Light the four candles and place each in its correct position on the compass to form the shape of a cross, with the white quartz crystal in the center.

To invoke the help of the guardian angels associated with the Four Winds, chant the spell (opposite) while you make the bracelet using a Four-strand Flat Plait (see page 123). If you finish the chant before you complete the braid, just keep repeating it until the bracelet is done.

Tie the ends of the braid together with a Reef Knot (see page 121), or another knot of your choice, then blow out the candles, thank the angels for their help, and wear the bracelet to promote good friendship and beneficial social energy between you.

WHEN TO
CAST SPELL
Whenever you
socialize, or want
to affirm new
or re-establish
old bonds

"To Uriel's North I pledge my trust
To find me love for all of us.
To Michael's South I pray for love
For all my friends give kindly doves.
To Raphael, my Eastern light
Bring empathy and wisdom bright.
My last to Gabriel, my Western star
The one who brings us golden chance."

Stairway to Happy Family Life—
Knot-seeing

We all have some kind of family—whether parents, children,
relatives, or just some kind of clan or group—that we belong
to. This spell imbues you and all those who are involved in
your "family" with a sense of belonging to one another or,
at the least, being there for each other come rain or shine.

The illustration on the opposite page
shows a spiral staircase rising up
to the Sun in the sky and on each
of the five steps are items traditionally
symbolic of happiness and harmony. For this
visualization technique you are simply going
to imagine yourself climbing the staircase
and knotting each item on each step with a
length of golden thread, thus joining them
together. Once you have performed the
ritual, simply say the incantation (opposite)
for the magic to work.

At the first step is a bouquet of roses, a
motif for generosity and giving. As you tie
the imaginary knot, see yourself giving a
bouquet of flowers to everyone you want
to be happy.

At the second step is a dragonfly brooch.
The dragonfly is a symbol of peace and love
in many Eastern traditions. Here, as you tie
the knot, see yourself pinning the brooch to
the person you want to be happy and well.

On the third step is an ancient key. As you
tie the key into the golden thread, imagine
it is the key to opening the door to a better
future for all of your family.

On the fourth step is a small jewelry
box. As you imagine looping and tying the
golden thread around the little chest, put
good thoughts inside it too, such as "love,"
"opportunity," "wealth," "peace," "kindness,"
and so on.

On the last step is a lotus flower, which
is an Eastern symbol of spiritual happiness.
This is to bless all of your family in your
thoughts as you knot it into your golden
thread.

Now you look up to the sky and finally
tie the end of the thread to the Sun's rays in
order to connect you and all of your family to
solar energy.

Repeat the incantation.

WHEN TO CAST SPELL

Just after sunrise to welcome positive solar energy into your family life

"With love and blessing all be done,
The golden thread has tied our love
And each of us a new day comes,
Where we are one, blessed from the Sun."

Witches' Ladder for a Bountiful Family or Clan

If you want your family to benefit from an abundant life, or to receive or seek great opportunities, as well as yourself, then this witches' ladder will promote the sacred energy of bountiful bird totems.

Among the indigenous peoples of North America, birds' feathers—particularly the raven's—were considered sacred and often used in ceremonies to give thanks to specific deities for a bountiful harvest, hunt, or battle won. The Iroquois peoples, for example, celebrated with a Feather Dance, in which ravens' feathers were attached to clothes, placed in the hair, or used to adorn horses and other animals during a grand festival to worship the gods.

WHAT YOU WILL NEED

2–3ft (60–90cm) length of cord, ribbon, or twine

10 large black feathers

10 dried red chilis

Sandalwood incense sticks

Rose quartz crystal

SPELL CASTING

Using Multiple Overhand Knots (see page 122), knot the black feathers, red chilis, and sandalwood sticks (which are symbolic of acceptance, growth, and harmony) into your length of cord, ribbon, or twine. As you knot in the items, repeat the charm (opposite) until the ladder is complete. Tie off the ends, then hang the ladder in the window of your kitchen or in a main hallway. Place the rose quartz crystal nearby to generate and maximize its loving power.

WHEN TO
CAST SPELL
Just before the
Full Moon

"With feathers black and chilis red
My clan is found, acceptance said.
With gratitude to those above
Now bountiful we bless the gods."

Blood Knot for Loyalty and Trust

Although we love and cherish family and friends, we also worry at times about how much we can trust others and how loyal they actually are to us. To ensure that you can share your secrets with others, or reveal your fears and woes, use this spell to make sure you are in trusted company.

The power of this spell is maximized by using a "blood knot" to enhance all aspects of "blood" ties. Blood ties (i.e. family ties) were deemed important in most traditional cultures worldwide to maintain the growth of a clan, family, or people.

WHAT YOU WILL NEED

Length of red cord, string, or ribbon

Piece of paper and pencil (to draw the Magic Circle opposite)

SPELL CASTING

Take the length of cord, string, or ribbon and make a Blood Knot (see page 125). Draw the Magic Circle on a piece of paper and write the following lines around the circle:

"Blood for trust and blood for love."

Place the knot in the center of the circle, and repeat the line five times to petition the spell to the Universe and ensure long-term loyalty from all concerned.

Repeat the chant below, then wrap the knot in the paper and keep it in a safe place.

"Blood brothers, sisters, family now
We trust this universal vow
To keep us safe from outer harm
Now ties are knotted for this charm."

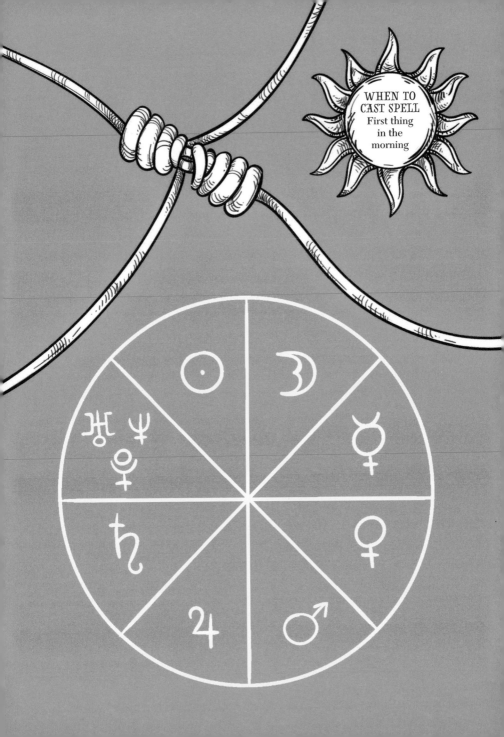

WHEN TO
CAST SPELL
First thing
in the
morning

Forget-Me-Knot— Keeping a Friend Spell

Our best friends can become long-distant pals, rivals, or even enemies. One of you meets a new lover; one of you becomes dedicated to a job; or maybe even one of you moves abroad?

This spell will ensure that whatever the challenge you face, you will remain friends in spite of it all. Friendship or kinship is about respect and acceptance, and that soulful empathy of always being there for each other, however long it is before you see one another again or however far apart you grow through changing circumstances.

WHAT YOU WILL NEED

Length of string, twine, or ribbon (long enough to tie at least seven overhand knots)

Gold or silver ring

Small silk pouch (or purse)

Forget-me-not (or an image of the flower)

Rose essential oil

SPELL CASTING

Sit in a quiet, comfortable place and begin to tie your overhand knots. As you do so, repeat the lines (opposite) for each of the knots.

Pull the knotted length through the ring, then tie the ends together to form a loop. Place the knotted ring in the pouch, along with the forget-me-not.

Leave the pouch overnight on a window ledge or other place where it will be directly aligned to the energy of the Moon, but only after you have sanctified it with a few drops of rose oil and said:

"Thank you Universe for blessing this sealed friendship forever."

Next day, place the pouch in a secret drawer, knowing that your friendship will be true forever.

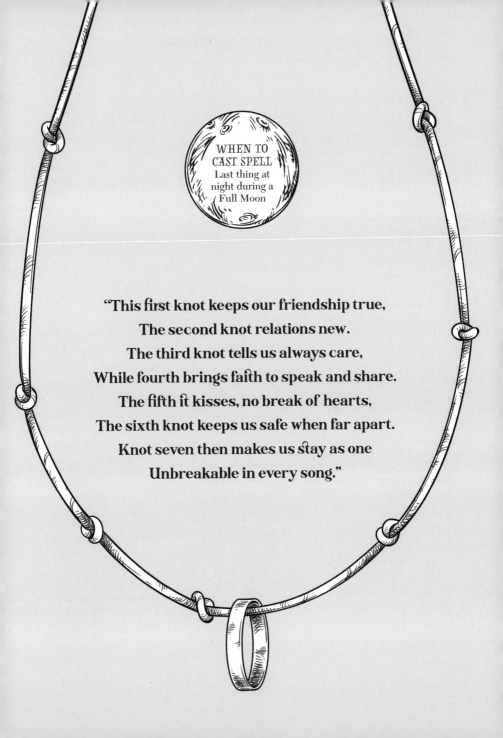

"This first knot keeps our friendship true,
The second knot relations new.
The third knot tells us always care,
While fourth brings faith to speak and share.
The fifth it kisses, no break of hearts,
The sixth knot keeps us safe when far apart.
Knot seven then makes us stay as one
Unbreakable in every song."

Spell for Restoring a Difficult Family Relationship

Of course, there are times when we don't get on with family members. We didn't choose them consciously as our friends. Perhaps the relationship is impossible to maintain because we have different beliefs, lifestyles, or needs. Sometimes we just can't understand or accept the other person and their dreams or desires.

This old European ribbon charm enables you to repair a dysfunctional relationship, or at least to compromise and accept your differences. It doesn't mean you have to become wed to your family, just that you and they can agree to differ.

WHAT YOU WILL NEED

3 white ribbons

4 yellow candles

Lighter or matches

Yellow ribbon (long enough to wrap around most of the length of finished braid)

Tea tree oil

SPELL CASTING

Fix the three white ribbons securely to a post or door handle, or attach them to a flat surface. Then light the candles for added protection from any psychic negativity from family members. Place one to the North of you, one to the South, one to the West, and one to the East.

Make a simple three-cord braid with the white ribbons and tie off at both ends. Wind the yellow ribbon round and round the braid until it is bound. Anoint the yellow ribbon with a few drops of tea tree oil, then tie tightly at both ends. As you do so, say the enchantment (opposite).

Next time you meet the family member who is proving difficult, carry the totem with you and the energy of the bound ribbons will create a positive rapport.

"All negative energy be gone from our life
All thoughts be good and true.
Whatever is broken is now restored
With ribbons for me and you.
From now and ever this family token
Will never again be broken

So mote it be."

WHEN TO
CAST SPELL
Sunny
morning

CHAPTER THREE

Career & Lifestyle

SPELLS

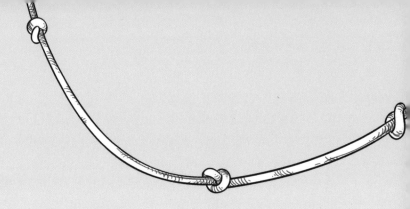

Not everyone is driven by a full-time career. Some of us may long for a more spiritual or nature-oriented existence, but many others seek a real sense of vocation. This sense of "calling" is often overlooked due to family or societal expectations. So, if your career or job doesn't fulfil you or give you joy in any way, then maybe it's time to discover a new pathway to go down? Whether you're looking to build an empire, find a sense of vocation, or simply lead a more leisurely lifestyle, this chapter provides you with all the magic needed to set your goals and manifest your quest.

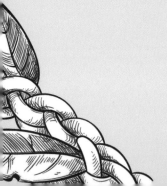

Key-to-the-Door Knot— For Job Success

Whether it's going for a new job interview or feeling proud of an achievement, or for admiration, praise, and reward for what you do, this knotted enchantment will bring you the success you deserve.

In feng shui, the ancient Eastern art of placement of items and objects in the home, there is one old ritual using the placement of keys to enhance all forms of success in your work. This knotted enchantment uses seven keys because seven is an auspicious Chinese number for job success.

WHAT YOU WILL NEED

Length of twine (thin enough to thread through the keys)

7 very old metal keys

SPELL CASTING

Take the length of twine and tie seven knots along its length. Hold each knot in turn while you repeat the charm (opposite).

Hold up the two ends of the knotted twine, thread the keys on one by one, and tie at the top. Hang the enchantment on a door handle or attach it to a wall nearest your main entrance. The seven knots will promote positive energy to exit the door with you, while the seven keys will unlock new opportunities and open the doors to success. Just before you go for an interview or ask for a change in your job routine, repeat the charm as you hold each key in turn in your hand.

WHEN TO
CAST SPELL
Waxing Moon

"With knot one my will be done
With knot two I'll get success.
Three knots down and here's my best
While four brings new keys to my door
And opening them will gain me more.
Knot five for achievement
And six for gold.
The seventh will make
My success be bold."

Bay Leaf Witches' Ladder to Seal a Deal

In contemporary living, there are many ways to seal a deal. This can be something empowering, such as a promotion, an opportunity to seize success, or for completion of a project or campaign.

Like other witches' ladders, the ritual of weaving totems into a braid maximizes the power and intention of the spell. This particular braid was often woven by ancient Greek ladies to ensure that their husbands would ride safely into battle. The braids were then hung from the pommel of the horses' saddles or from shields or weapons as a reminder that these warriors were winners. Here's how to be a winner yourself.

WHAT YOU WILL NEED

4 x 3ft (90cm) lengths of thin cord (one yellow, one blue, one green, and one red— these colors correspond to the four elements which protect you)

16 bay leaves (four for each of the four elements)

Piece of paper and pencil (for writing down the seal-a-deal intention)

SPELL CASTING

Follow the instructions for making a Four-strand Flat Plait (see page 123). After you have woven the braid, tie it off at the end and insert the bay leaves wherever you like.

Repeat the spell (opposite) as you write it down on a piece of paper.

Place the braided bay leaves near your desk or workspace, and each time you pass by touch a leaf for luck and to energize your ability to seal any deal.

In the morning, or just before you want to make an impact

"By herbs and braid this deal be done
By Fire and Earth, request is won.
By Water and Air, my winnings be
This braid my truth of mastery."

Knots and Crystals Better Lifestyle Spell

There are as many different kinds of lifestyles as there are individuals. Some of us want a laid-back life; others wish to immerse themselves in business, money, pleasure, or excitement.

We witchy folk often use crystals as an empowering way to enhance and energize the intention and purpose of our spells. This particular enchantment is hugely dependent on the power of three crystals—citrine, aventurine, and malachite. If you can't get hold of these crystals, I suggest you find a beautiful image of each crystal instead and stick these on the mirror that you also need for this charm.

WHAT YOU WILL NEED

3 candles (one dark green, one yellow, and one light green, to reinforce the energy of the crystals)

Lighter or matches

Wall mirror

Piece of malachite

Piece of citrine

Piece of aventurine

3ft (90cm) length of ribbon

SPELL CASTING

Light the three candles and arrange them in a triangular shape, with the yellow candle at the top beside the mirror. Next, place the corresponding crystal next to each candle—so, the malachite next to the dark green candle; the citrine next to the yellow candle; and the aventurine next to the light green candle. Sit facing the mirror and start to make your knot spell.

Say the enchantment (opposite) as you make nine knots in your length of ribbon.

Encircle the knotted ribbon around the triangle of crystals and candles. Repeat the spell and gently blow out each of the candles. Keep the ribbon in a safe place with the crystals. Believe in your spell, and you will have the lifestyle you are truly looking for.

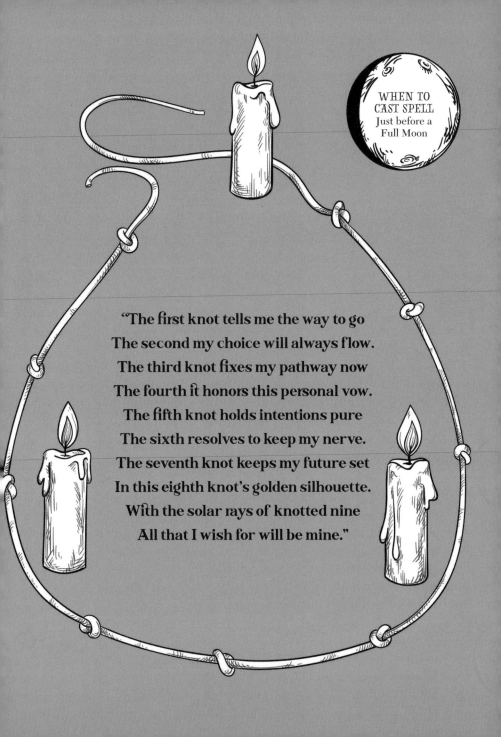

"The first knot tells me the way to go
The second my choice will always flow.
The third knot fixes my pathway now
The fourth it honors this personal vow.
The fifth knot holds intentions pure
The sixth resolves to keep my nerve.
The seventh knot keeps my future set
In this eighth knot's golden silhouette.
With the solar rays of knotted nine
All that I wish for will be mine."

Gordian Knot— Letting Go of the Past

We may be obsessed with what the future holds, but before we can get to grips with new lifestyles or big changes, we need to let go of anything from the past that is holding us back. This spell does exactly that.

An ancient Greek myth tells of how the poor peasant, Gordius, was mistakenly thought to be the next king of Phrygia, and so to honor Zeus he dedicated his ox-cart by tying it to the god's statue with a knot that could never be undone.

Many hundreds of years later, infamous Alexander the Great solved the puzzle by simply cutting through the knot with his sword. In a way, this was cheating a bit, but sometimes, similarly, we have to unravel life's knots and sometimes cut through them metaphorically too. This action dissipates negative energy so that we can move on. This knot charm will help you do that.

This time, you're going to make a Monkey Braid, but without tying off the ends, and then unravel the braid to release you from the past.

WHAT YOU WILL NEED

3 x 3ft (90cm) lengths of cord or string

3 pieces of white quartz crystal

SPELL CASTING

Make three Monkey Braids (see page 118) from the lengths of cord or string, but don't tie off the ends. Place the braids vertically on a table to make three lines. Above each of the lines, place a piece of white quartz to maximize the energy.

Take up the first crystal and repeat the first enchantment (opposite). Now take the ends of the braid and pull on them until you just have one long piece of cord or string again. Take up the next piece of crystal and repeat the second enchantment. Do the same with the second braid.

Finally, take up the last piece of crystal, say the third enchantment out loud, and do the same with the third braid.

Take the three strings or cords, tie each one round the crystals—knotting them however you like—and keep in a safe place for a brilliant, crystallized future.

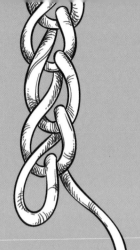

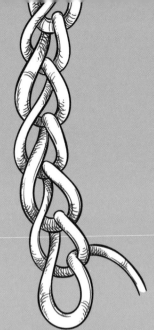

ENCHANTMENT 2
"With this braid
untied, all that
has been will no
longer hurt me."

ENCHANTMENT 3
"With this braid
unknotted, all that
was not right for
me will never be in
my life again."

ENCHANTMENT 1
"With this braid
untied, my life
will change for
the better."

WHEN TO CAST SPELL

Just before
a New Moon

Attract Helpful People for a Better Career

Tying knots in lengths of fabric was thought by ancient Eastern mystics to attract useful mentors when worn on your person. This simple spell will enhance all positive contacts in your life.

I n Eastern feng shui, the Northwest part of your home is associated with mentors and helpful people. This is where you are going to perform the spell. So, if you're not sure where that is, get hold of a compass to check.

WHAT YOU WILL NEED

5 red candles

Lighter or matches

5 coins of any denomination (to represent the five elements in Chinese astrology)

Large silk scarf (red is best, but any color is fine)

SPELL CASTING

Light the candles in a circle and place the five coins in a row in front of you. Take up the silk scarf and tie a knot in each corner, repeating the chant below as you do so:

"With these knots I make it clear to bring support and mentors dear."

Now lay the scarf flat on the table and place the coins, one by one, in the center. As you do this, say the enchantment (opposite).

Tie the four corners of the scarf together with one big knot, so that the coins are contained in your "scarf bag." Place the bag in the Northwest corner of your home to enhance and attract good contacts for as long as you require them.

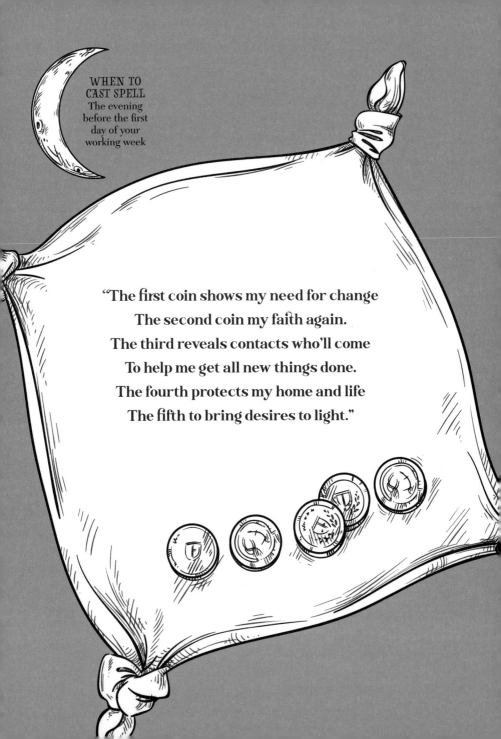

WHEN TO
CAST SPELL
The evening
before the first
day of your
working week

"The first coin shows my need for change
The second coin my faith again.
The third reveals contacts who'll come
To help me get all new things done.
The fourth protects my home and life
The fifth to bring desires to light."

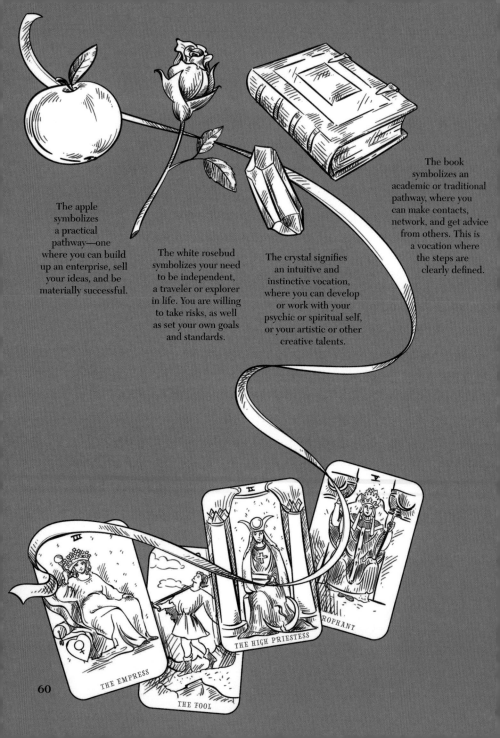

The apple symbolizes a practical pathway—one where you can build up an enterprise, sell your ideas, and be materially successful.

The white rosebud symbolizes your need to be independent, a traveler or explorer in life. You are willing to take risks, as well as set your own goals and standards.

The crystal signifies an intuitive and instinctive vocation, where you can develop or work with your psychic or spiritual self, or your artistic or other creative talents.

The book symbolizes an academic or traditional pathway, where you can make contacts, network, and get advice from others. This is a vocation where the steps are clearly defined.

THE EMPRESS

THE FOOL

THE HIGH PRIESTESS

ROPHANT

Knot-seeing Enchantment Vocation Decision

The Tarot has been used for centuries as a divination tool, but also for making crucial decisions about the future. This knot-seeing visualization ritual will enable you to clarify which pathway you really want to go down.

The four cards on the opposite page—the Empress, the Fool, the High Priestess, and the Hierophant—are all symbolic of certain types of vocation.

Close your eyes and relax somewhere calm and quiet. Imagine you are walking through a lush forest, carrying a basket to forage for wild fruits or herbs. You meet the Empress who represents abundant pleasure. As you walk toward her, she offers you a golden apple and you are tempted by the joys it could bring you. You refuse at first, but the Empress appears to offer material pleasure, so you place it in your basket and thank her.

As you walk on, a young man bumps into you as he looks up at the cloudless sky. This is the Fool. He represents freedom and the unpredictable. He apologizes and offers you a white rosebud and you take it without even thinking, so struck are you by his carefree spirit. He is gone before you can thank him.

As you wander on, you meet the High Priestess, gazing across the horizon. She symbolizes intuition and all things secret or unknown. She holds out her hand in friendship and gives you a white quartz. You take it gratefully and begin to thank her,

but she puts her finger to her lips as if to say, "Shhh" and so you nod and walk on.

Lastly, you meet the Hierophant, a man dressed in robes, who seems worldly-wise and guru-like. He carries a staff and points the way forward for you, as if he knows which path you want to go down. He represents stability, mentors, wise counsel, and traditional values. You thank him for showing you the way, and he gives you a small book of wisdom.

Along with the four objects in your basket, you also have a long white ribbon, and it's time to sit down to make a choice. Imagine you place each item on the ground before you—the apple, the rosebud, the crystal, and the book, and now you have to choose which of these literally calls to you.

Whichever one it is, imagine knotting the white ribbon around it, putting it back in your basket, and leaving the other items behind as you continue on your journey. Now open your eyes and see which vocational pathway you are going to follow.

Dream Vocation Spell

Once we have chosen our vocation or career, we know that there may be obstacles, be they financial or personal difficulties or just life's little upsets thrown our way. To make sure you have a smoother ride to fulfilling your dream vocation, use this "cabinet of curiosities" charm.

Medieval European kings and nobles were big fans of collecting the most bizarre objects which they placed in a beautiful cabinet and showed off to visiting dignitaries. Rather like owning holy relics, it implied they were powerful, wise, and worth knowing. Curious objects, magic potions, and other symbolic artefacts were also collected by physicians, academics, and Freemasons, such as politician and alchemist, Elias Ashmole.

With this spell you're going to create your own collection of magical empowerment items and seal your intention for a successful vocation with one simple knot.

WHAT YOU WILL NEED

A selection of shells, beads, stones, and pebbles

Onyx, malachite, citrine, and red jade

White candle

Lighter or matches

Large glass jar with a lid

Cinnamon essential oil

Clove essential oil

Ginger essential oil

Black velvet ribbon

SPELL CASTING

Gather together all your ingredients, place them on a table, and light the candle. Gaze into the empty jar for a few minutes (with the candle behind it) and visualize yourself doing exactly what your vocation is all about. Keep imagining yourself in that role and see all the things you want to achieve.

One by one, take up the items in your collection and place them in the jar, choosing the smallest items first and finishing with the four crystals. Scatter four drops of each of the oils onto the crystals as you repeat the enchantment (opposite).

Seal the jar by tying and knotting the black ribbon around it, then leave in a special place in your home where no one can touch it.

Whenever you feel you need to boost your motivational spirit, open the jar and hold each of the crystals to enhance success in your vocation.

Only when you know exactly
what career or vocation you
are embarking upon

"This jar is filled
With all that I wish to be.
My vocational future
Is now guaranteed."

Self-empowerment and Charisma Spell to Create Your Own Future

It's hard these days to know what we truly want for our future, isn't it? This spell will not only empower you with charisma and self-confidence, but enable you to create the future you truly desire right now.

The ancient Egyptians were dedicated to many gods, but one of the most important was the sun-god, Ra. Earliest worshippers considered Ra to be a creator god from whose tears mankind was made. In later dynasties, he was thought to travel the skies in a golden barge by day and by night his boat would descend to the Underworld until he returned in the morning to bring light to the world again. This spell will draw on the sun-god's potent, inspiring energy of creative empowerment, and make charisma all your own.

WHAT YOU WILL NEED

5 gold rings

5 lengths of gold-colored ribbon or cord

SPELL CASTING

On a very sunny morning, lay the five gold rings in a circle, either outside in full sunlight or in a very sunny place indoors. Take the five lengths of ribbon or cord, and tie five knots in each one. Place each knotted length in a spiral on top of a ring and leave for 24 hours.

As you place the knotted lengths on the rings, repeat the enchantment (opposite). When you return the next day to remove the rings and knotted lengths, say, as you touch each ring:

"One for creative joy
Two for self-empowerment
Three for charisma
Four for thanks to the gods
Five for unending self-confidence."

Take the rings and knotted lengths, and leave them in a safe, secret place. Take them out and repeat the spell whenever you want to augment your charisma and confidence.

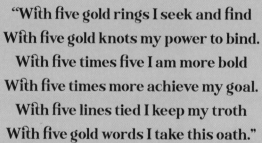

"With five gold rings I seek and find
With five gold knots my power to bind.
With five times five I am more bold
With five times more achieve my goal.
With five lines tied I keep my troth
With five gold words I take this oath."

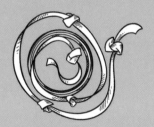

CHAPTER FOUR

Prosperity & Abundance

SPELLS

Whether you are seeking material or psycho-spiritual wealth, this collection of spells will bring you all the opportunity and luck you need. However, remember always to know exactly how much you want of something before you ask for it. It's no good just saying I want more money or a bigger house. The Universe doesn't know what more and bigger are in relation to your needs. So, if you have $50 and want $100, then say, "I would like a hundred dollars in total, please." Don't be greedy, though! The Universe is only generous to those who are kind, modest, and care about everyone else's wealth too.

Counting Knots
For Prosperity

This quick and easy spell can be worked with a shoelace. So, if you're looking for a bit of financial luck, or to attract prosperity, then get knotting with anything you can lay your hands on.

To acquire wealth in whatever shape or form, follow the wise merchants of ancient China who, once they had counted out their coins (the ones with square holes in the middle), would string them together to make it easy to carry them around and for counting out when trading or making transactions. In Chinese numerology, nine is a highly auspicious number, and is considered to be the number of wealth and success. Because you may not have access to Chinese coins with holes, this spell includes coinage as an added boost to your prosperity empowerment.

WHAT YOU WILL NEED

2ft (60cm) length of yellow cord or ribbon

9 coins

Small silk pouch (or purse)

SPELL CASTING

Tie the cord or ribbon to a post or door handle, or attach to a stable surface, and repeat the complete incantation (opposite) as you make a series of nine overhand knots—this really gets you focusing the energy into the knots every time you make one.

When you have finished, repeat the charm once more as you hold the last knot in your hand and thank the Universe for attracting the gift of prosperity to you. Keep the knotted cord or ribbon in a pouch with the nine coins in order to reinforce your spell.

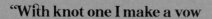
"With knot one I make a vow

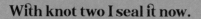
With knot two I seal it now.

With knot three this charm preserve
To bring me all that I deserve.

With knot four I see the light
Of wealth and goodness that's my right.

With knot five believe it's true
This spell to grant me blessings too.

With knot six success is mine

With knot seven my vision's fine.

With knot eight my charm is done

For with knot nine my fortune's won."

Abundant Lifestyle Charm

Abundance isn't just about money; it can be about abundant friends, work, or creative inspiration. In whatever way you want to enrich your life, this charm will attract it to you.

In many Far Eastern and ancient civilizations, rice was thought to be both sacred to the gods and beneficial to our prosperity. To enhance your petition to the Universe, use nine knots and nine grains of sacred white rice. Think carefully what you want more of before you start knotting. If you want more money, exactly how much do you want? If you want more free time or abundant inspiration, then say exactly how much you want of whatever commodity it is. It's no good asking the Universe for more money because more could be five cents or $500,000. It's all relative. So, decide exactly what you want before you start the spell.

WHAT YOU WILL NEED

Yellow candle (for abundance)

Lighter or matches

Piece of paper and pencil

9 grains of white rice

2ft (60cm) length of white cord

SPELL CASTING

Light the candle and write down exactly what you want on a piece of paper. Place the nine grains of rice in a circle around your written testament.

Take up your cord and make nine simple knots. As you do so, say the enchantment (opposite).

Place the knotted cord in a circle around the rice circle, gaze into the candle flame for a few moments focusing on your desired goal, then blow out the candle and leave the cord, rice, and paper in a safe place until the Full Moon, so your wish can be fulfilled.

WHEN TO
CAST SPELL
During the
evening on a New
Crescent Moon

"With rice and cord I seal and secure

For more of what's been written here."

Witches' Ladder Basil Booster for Financial Gain

This four-braid witches' ladder will ensure that whatever way financial gain arrives, it will bring you the joy of more security and a lifestyle which is stress-free.

We all want financial relief, fewer burdens, less debt, more to spend, and the sense of security this can apparently give us. Although more money can bring more stress, this spell is simply to make you feel good about your finances and to attract better financial stability to you. The route that this security comes to you may not be via a lottery win, an inheritance, or a lump sum; it might be that you find attracting this kind of gain comes from hard work or economic changes. Basil has long been used to purify and protect, but also to prevent financial loss and to boost your ability to attract positive money-making opportunities.

WHAT YOU WILL NEED

4 x 3–4ft (90–120cm) lengths of natural jute or hemp twine

A selection of shells and beads (to thread onto the twine)

A selection of Chinese coins (the ones with square holes)

Fresh basil leaves

A few teaspoons of dried basil

SPELL CASTING

Start your Four-strand Flat Plait (see page 123) by tying the ends of the twine together and attaching to a solid support. As you weave the twine, thread on the shells, beads, and coins, and insert the basil leaves where you feel appropriate. As you get a rhythm going, you will begin to know when the moment is right to add each of your ingredients. Tie off at the end.

Repeat the charm (opposite) while you sprinkle the dried basil over the completed length of your witches' ladder.

Hang the ladder near your front door, desk, or work space to promote financial success.

WHEN TO
CAST SPELL
Just after a
New Moon

"By will, determination, and design
This ladder is my cash lifeline
To take me to a place secure
Where all I want is less or more
Where I can live with peace of mind
For then what comes is gain in time."

Chinese Dragon Charm for Good Fortune

This ancient Chinese dragon charm will enable you to overcome all obstacles until you feel you are truly fortunate. It will enhance energy and ambition, and attract good times into all aspects of your life.

To the Chinese, abundance comes in many packages. Shrewd Chinese merchants who traded in spices, exquisite porcelain, jade dragons, and gemstones knew the very things they sold were a sign of their own good fortune. Jade is one of those stones which is associated with happiness and success, while dragons in Chinese mythology represent prosperity, good luck, and fortunate circumstances. Fucanglong was the Chinese mythical dragon who guarded hidden treasures, such as gemstones, gold, and the riches of nature. He is said to create a volcano as he bursts from the ground to show off his bounty to the heavenly gods. His most prized possession is a wish-fulfilling pearl.

WHAT YOU WILL NEED

5 strands of red silk thread

5 pieces of jade (light green is best)

The dragon image (as drawn opposite)

SPELL CASTING

Using the image of the dragon on the opposite page, you are going to welcome good fortune into your life.

Take each red silk thread in turn and make one overhand knot in the middle. As you do so, repeat the following charm:

*"Red silk so knotted let it be
To bring good fortune back to me."*

Take the five pieces of jade and place them around the dragon.

Finally, take the five red threads and knot them all together in the middle. Sprawl the threads out in a fiery circle over the dragon image with the central knot over the pearl, then say the spell (opposite).

Keep the jade pieces and the knotted threads on a window ledge where there is maximum sunshine for one lunar cycle to activate the charm.

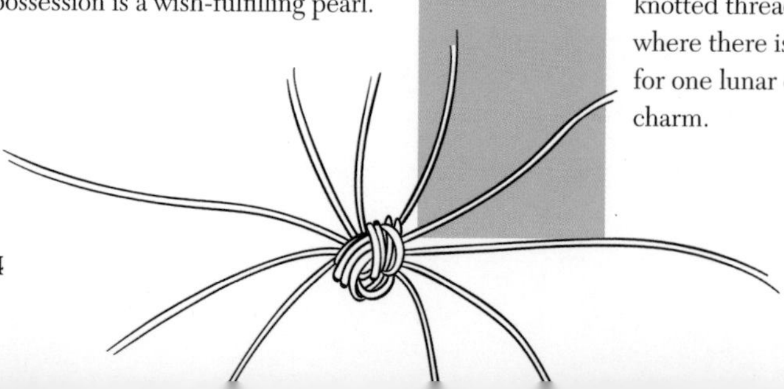

WHEN TO
CAST SPELL
A sunny
morning

"With dragon power and dragon fire
My fortune's set to my desire.
This wishing pearl makes dreams come true
For good times, luck, and success too."

Enchantment for Prosperous Living

This is a visualization spell for enhancing all negotiations and plans for a better future. Whether you want to be prosperous in mind or material possessions, or rich in spirit, you will soon find the kind of luck you're looking for comes your way.

Throughout ancient worldwide civilizations, gods and goddesses were worshipped and petitioned to bring favor to one's life. In ancient Greece, for example, the planets (the then known ones) and stars were considered to be embodiments of these deities. Under the night sky, they were blessed and appeased to ensure good harvests or prosperous living. The gods Hermes, Aphrodite, Ares, Kronos, and Zeus were the earliest major deities in Greek religious belief, and were represented by the planets Mercury, Venus, Mars, Saturn, and Jupiter.

On the opposite page are the planets in the night sky, surrounded by twinkling stars, and a heavenly necklace made of moonstones. The goddess of the Moon, Selene, leaves this trail of moonbeams every night as she glides across the heavens and by morning it is gone, as the sun-god, Helios, returns to lighten the world. This is your chance to take the magic necklace and wrap it around all the planets to empower you with their energy.

Gaze at the image and imagine you are riding through the constellations on a golden chariot. As you travel closer to the planets, you reach out for the moonstone necklace and begin to wind it round and round each of the planets, and, finally, you tie the end to your chariot to carry their energy with you wherever you go. Repeat this visualization to enhance all aspects of prosperous living.

WHEN TO
CAST SPELL
Night of a
Full Moon

Goal Charm

This spell is used for one specific goal you have in life.
It could be simply to be successful, to have a better lifestyle,
to attract helpful contacts, or to improve communication,
or just to ensure you have a truly creative lifestyle.

This spell uses sunflower seeds, a yellow candle, and citrine, which are all associated with bright, positive energy. In Greek mythology, one myth tells of Apollo, the god of light, who rode his golden chariot across the skies by day and was loved by numerous nymphs. One water nymph, Clytie, was charmed by him, but her love was unrequited. She couldn't take her eyes off Apollo and for months she lay upon a barren rock watching his chariot sail through the sky, her head turning to follow his path all day long. She eventually died without food or water, so the gods turned her into a sunflower, which still turns its head to follow the sun, from morning until night.

WHAT YOU WILL NEED

Short yellow candle

Lighter or matches

2 yellow, silk, three-strand braids

Sunflower image (as drawn opposite)

A handful of sunflower seeds

SPELL CASTING

With this spell, you are going to knot beneficial solar light into your life and ensure your goal is realized. Whatever it is you are seeking, make sure it is an exact goal, composed of only a short sentence or a one-word idea. This is because you are going to have to write it as a petition to the Universe on the yellow candle.

Carve the yellow candle with your goal, then say the charm (opposite).

Next, light the candle and tie a knot in the middle of each of your two lengths of braid (already knotted at the start and finish). Let the candle burn down into your petition as it rises in the smoke to the Universe, then blow it out.

On the image of the sunflower on the opposite page, scatter the sunflower seeds and place the two knotted braids in the form of a cross over the flower. Leave the knots and the seeds on the open page for one complete day to maximize the power of the solar energy.

"I write my request on this candle to bring me light,
to reinforce the power of the sun in my life,
and to manifest my goal."

Conjure Bag for Good Contacts

We all need favorable contacts and useful allies. To ensure
you can trust and rely on them, collect a selection of magic
ingredients, place them in a conjure bag, and soon you will
have all the help you need to create a successful future.

Conjure bags are also known as Mojo bags in voodoo. Thousands of years ago, the ancient Egyptians filled small pouches with gold leaves, jewel-encrusted talismans, and amulets to ensure the safe passage of their loved ones' souls on their journey to the afterlife. The amulets also ensured the soul would be welcomed by other kind souls when they arrived. The ankh, the Egyptian symbol of the morning Sun and eternal life, will also invoke positive energy among mentors and welcome kind and generous souls into your life. So, make yourself a conjure bag and carry it with you whenever you need to encourage good contacts into your life.

WHAT YOU WILL NEED

Length of black leather or silk cord

An ankh (cut from cardstock or kraft paper if necessary)

3 pieces of citrine

Cinnamon stick

3 cloves

Sandalwood essential oil

Red silk pouch (or purse)

SPELL CASTING

First make the knotted ankh by threading the cord through the top of the ankh and then making a strong Surgeon's Knot (see page 124) to tie it off.

Before you place all the items in the pouch, you need to anoint and cast a spell over them.

Lay the knotted ankh and other items on a table and sprinkle everything with a few drops of sandalwood oil. As you do so, say:

"With this magic pouch
my future's sure,
For all that come
will open new doors."

Place the items, one by one, in the pouch, with the knotted ankh going in last, as you say the enchantment (opposite).

Sprinkle a few more drops of sandalwood oil into the pouch, close it up, and take it with you whenever you want special help from contacts.

WHEN TO
CAST SPELL
First thing in
the morning

"With friends to come and allies fine

This pouch invokes amazing times.

Give thanks to those who fuel my life

With wise words and support divine."

CHAPTER FIVE

Protection &
Spiritual Healing

SPELLS

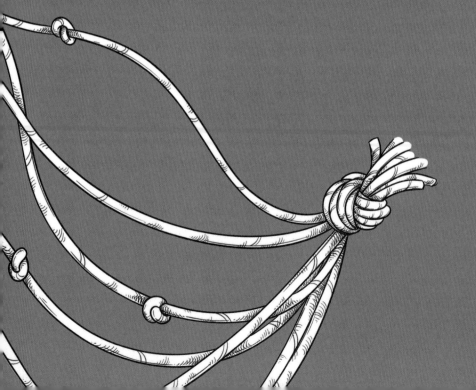

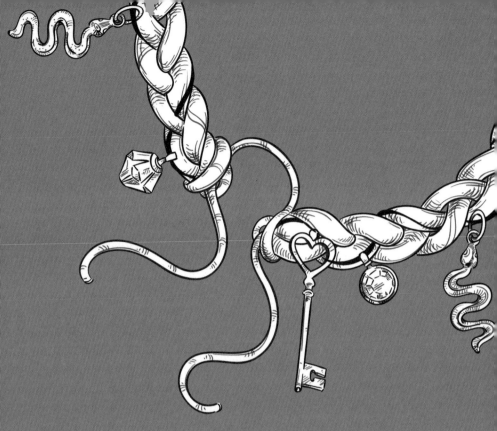

Negative energy comes in many forms out there in the big wide world. There's environmental and geopathic stress; unpleasant and harmful psychic energy from people around us; and unwelcome spiritual footprints left by those who have passed on. We might also need to heal or develop our own sense of spiritual self, or protect ourselves and others from someone else's bad thoughts and banish them from our lives. This chapter of spells will help you to nurture, protect, and keep secure your sacred self.

Mirror and Moon Protection Charm

Out in the big wide world, many of us are acutely sensitive to the geopathic energies around us. But this simple, highly effective charm will protect you from environmental stress by drawing on the protective powers of the Moon.

I n ancient Egypt, the moon goddess, Hathor, presided over magic. She was worshipped and given thanks for her power to protect and guide us through all aspects of life. In her honor, mirrors were made out of copper (her sacred metal), and when a devotee gazed at their reflection, they absorbed her magical power of protection. In civilizations such as Greek, Roman, Mesopotamian, and Chinese, mirrors were made of reflective materials such as bronze or crystal. The mirror was also used to see into the future (the Aztecs were known for their obsidian scrying mirrors) and later by medieval sorcerers who left them out at night to draw down the protective power of the Moon.

WHAT YOU WILL NEED

White candle

Lighter or matches

Small handbag or makeup mirror

Pure spring water

Length of white ribbon

SPELL CASTING

To bring some much-needed protection from environmental influences, carry this lunar-charged magic mirror with you. With the reinforcement of the knotted ribbon to bind your intention of protection, it will deflect bad energy and invoke the Moon's power.

On the night of a Full Moon, light the white candle, then take your mirror and rinse under pure spring water to purify and bless it.

Take up the white ribbon and wind it round the mirror seven times, then tie it with any old knot. As you wind the ribbon round the mirror, say the charm (opposite).

Blow out the candle to petition your desire to the Moon, then leave the knotted mirror on a window ledge, or outside if necessary, for the whole night.

Next day, take the mirror with you in your handbag. It is advisable to re-empower the Moon's energy every few months.

WHEN TO
CAST SPELL
Full Moon

"Around and around and around I go
To wind this ribbon tight thus so.
With ribbon white my soul is safe
The lunar light reflects all else.
The goddess power is here for me
In all the places known to be.
This charm protected is myself
This mirror a virtue of good health."

A Charm for Spiritual Clarity

This spell amplifies and augments your Third Eye energy to bring spiritual clarity. Use the magical pentagram to bring truth to your spiritual self and to ensure it is in tune with the Universe.

The pentagram is a well-known symbol used in many religious faiths, including Christianity and the Bahai Faith, and also in more occult circles, such as among Freemasons, neopaganism, and Wiccan lore. The five-pointed star is usually shown with one triangle pointing skyward to emphasize connection with the spiritual world. When the pentagram is reversed, it is usually associated with darker magic. So, when you draw your pentagram, be sure to draw it exactly as shown and then you will be in touch with the universal power of spiritual oneness.

WHAT YOU WILL NEED

Large wall mirror

3 purple candles

Lighter or matches

3 purple cords or ribbons

Pentagram (as shown opposite)

Piece of parchment paper and pen

SPELL CASTING

In the evening, sit at a table in front of a mirror and light the three candles. Place one candle on either side of the mirror and the other between you and the mirror. Take up the three cords or ribbons and make three overhand knots along the lengths (these represent the body, spirit, and soul).

Draw your pentagram, as shown opposite, on the piece of parchment paper. Place the parchment in front of the mirror, then take the three cords or ribbons, and place one horizontally across the middle of the pentagram, one coiled in the center, and the third vertically across the middle of the pentagram. Say the enchantment (opposite).

This ritual spell, when performed regularly at every crescent Moon, will illuminate and amplify your spiritual connection to the Universe.

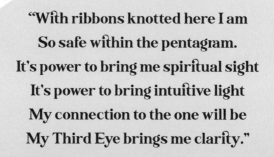

"With ribbons knotted here I am
So safe within the pentagram.
It's power to bring me spiritual sight
It's power to bring intuitive light
My connection to the one will be
My Third Eye brings me clarity."

Witches' Psychic Safety Ladder

Apart from geopathic stress and environmental pollution, we spend much of our time trying to accept, understand, or duck around other people's psychic negativity. To ensure that it doesn't rub off on you, create a witches' ladder to block and banish it from your life.

T housands of years ago, the ancient Greeks and Romans were highly superstitious and believed that others could curse them with invocations from the gods. Amulets were usually worn or carried to protect the wearer from harm. Another method was that certain magical items were knotted into strings of garlic (with its strong associations as a prevention against curses and hexing) and hung by a main entrance to secure, protect, and banish negativity. Nowadays, adverse intentions or the negative thinking of others, even if not directed at us, can cause us to feel edgy, stressed, or even worse, as if we are under some kind of curse. This witches' ladder will banish such bad projections forever.

WHAT YOU WILL NEED

6 x 3–4ft (90–120cm) black ribbons

6 x 1ft (30cm) red ribbons

Sprigs of lovage

A few fig leaves

A few bay leaves

A few white rosebuds

Garlic cloves or flowers

A few sprigs of lavender

5 pieces of rough black tourmaline

5 pieces of hematite

Jasmine essential oil

SPELL CASTING

Start by laying out all of the ingredients on your designated sacred place, table, or altar. Take the six black ribbons and make two three-strand braids. Bind the two black braids together using the red ribbons. Use simple bows to bind the black braids with two red ribbons at the top, two red ribbons in the middle, and two red ribbons at the bottom. Lay your ladder on the table and begin to insert the various pieces of foliage throughout, tying the tourmaline and hematite in with a bit of twine or fine thread to secure them. The crystals should be evenly arranged across the ladder. Finally, sprinkle the ladder with drops of jasmine oil to seal your intention. As you do so, repeat the spell (opposite).

Hang your ladder where you can blow it a kiss to bless it and for this protective device to bring you psychic protection every day.

"With woven ribbons black to banish
The red brings magic bold to vanquish.
To protect me from all negative thought
The rose and garlic from the fraught.
I bind my spell with fruits and leaves

That keep me safe when all deceive.
No stone unturned, these crystals black
Will every curse, spite, fear throw back.
I banish bad, but cast no harm
For I am safe when I make this charm."

Isis Knot Ritual for Enhanced Psychic Power

This ritual draws on the power of the Egyptian goddess Isis to protect, heal, and nurture your spiritual side. The spell also amplifies your psychic powers, such as intuition, divination, telepathy, and self-healing.

In Egyptian mythology, the "tyet," or knot of Isis, was supposedly a knotted girdle worn by the goddess Isis. It became a symbolic amulet, usually carved out of red jasper and placed in coffins to protect the soul of the dead. Similar knots were also tied into the robes of the priestesses of Isis and appeared in clothing in later Greek iconography. This Isis knot charm will enable you to reconnect to your deeper self and to elevate your psychic powers to a new level so that you are in tune with the spiritual world.

WHAT YOU WILL NEED

Tyet amulet (copy the amulet shown opposite on a piece of paper and color it red)

4 x 2ft (60cm) lengths of red cord

Red candle

Lighter or matches

SPELL CASTING

Find a quiet room and place the paper amulet in the center of the floor, with the four lengths of red cord surrounding it to make a square. Stand with the amulet square to the North of you and light your candle.

Hold the lit candle in your writing hand, then say the charm (opposite).

Repeat the above as you take up each cord in turn and make one simple overhand knot in the middle of the length.

Stand in the middle of the room, hold the candle, and focus on the flame, as you say:

"By the power of Isis and the magic of Isis I am protected through the binding of her girdle about me."

Blow out the candle when you are ready, and then finish by saying:

"Blessings to you, Isis, your magic is all around me."

WHEN TO
CAST SPELL
Full Moon

"By the power of Isis and the magic of Isis
I am healed by her first knot,
I am protected by her second knot,

I am awakened to my deeper self by her third knot,
I am at one with the Universe by her fourth knot."

Hecate's Unblocking Charm Bracelet

There are times when we feel stagnant. We don't progress and there always seems to be something stopping us from moving forward. This spell will unblock any kind of obstruction in your life and allow you to make destiny all your own.

Hecate was the Greek goddess of the boundary to the Underworld. She presided over thresholds, and was petitioned during the dark of the Moon when food was left at crossroads to honor her. Yet this hidden goddess will open up the road for you to see the crossroads as an opportunity rather than a dead end and also free you from any blockage on the spiritual or lifestyle road you're traveling on. Hecate is associated with the color black, night, keys, snakes, doorways, and dogs, yet she carries light hidden within her apparent darkness to show you the way with her torch.

WHAT YOU WILL NEED

3-strand braid made of fine black cord or ribbon (enough to make a bracelet), plus extra for tying

Fine black thread or cotton

3 old keys with holes

3 silver charm snakes or serpents

3 red crystal charms, such as jasper, carnelian, or ruby

3 black crystal charms, such as jet, ebony, or black tourmaline

Small silk pouch (or purse)

SPELL CASTING

To petition Hecate to protect you from obstacles in your life and to show you the way forward, bind your intention by knotting her sacred charms into this lucky bracelet. Make the braid as usual, and, as you do so, add the charms by knotting them into it using a separate fine thread or cotton. As you braid and add the charms, focus on what it is that needs unblocking in your life and what pathway you want to follow. Focus on how this spell will protect you, whichever pathway you to choose to go down.

Knot off the ends of the braid. To close the bracelet, loop a short length of cord or ribbon through each end of the braid knot, place the bracelet over your wrist, and tie the ends together in a Reef Knot (see page 121). Once you have made the bracelet, place it in a pouch for one night during the dark of the Moon, and then wear it accordingly. You will soon be free of any obstacles in your life.

WHEN TO CAST SPELL

Dark of the
New Moon

Aura Enchantment for Holistic Healing

Our aura, the invisible rainbow-like energy that radiates from us, can often be unbalanced due to psychological or physical influences. Use this knot spell to protect and re-balance your auric field and restore chakra wellbeing.

I n spiritual terms the aura is an expression of the universal energy, known in Eastern traditions as "chi" or "qi," which exudes from the human body. As it permeates all things, the emanations from our body literally color this energy depending on our state of being. Concentrated channels of this universal energy—the chakras—are focused at certain points of the body. These could be described as "the swing-doors" of the life-force flowing into and out of us. The chakras and the auric field are associated with various colors, thought to be seen in scientific imaging techniques and also by psychics. It is these colors that will boost and balance your aura's health.

WHAT YOU WILL NEED

7 x 3–4ft (90–120cm) lengths of cord in the following colors:

Red
Pink
Yellow
Green
Light blue
Violet
White

SPELL CASTING

Whether you can see them or not, balancing these seven colors of the aura will heal and balance your holistic state of being, too.

Take up the cords one at a time and make a big overhand knot in the center of each. As you do so, repeat the charm (opposite) for each color cord you pick up and knot.

After you knot each cord, lay it around your feet, so that at the end of the spell you are surrounded by, and standing in the center of, the seven colored cords. Take up each cord in the reverse order and knot them together at one end. Say:

"My aura is balanced now, and is protected by the power of universal energy that comes to me."

Keep the cords in a safe place, then, whenever you feel insecure, unhappy, or out of balance, take them out, unknot them, and repeat the spell to balance your aura.

"With red, I knot my passion pure

With pink, my love for others dear

With yellow, adapt and give out hope

With green, my poise is blessed and true

With blue, my spirited talents rise

With violet, my soulful side stays wise

With white, I'm empowered and whole again

With all, I am healed with this refrain."

Spiritual Healing Visualization

We often forget to look up at the stars or don't have time
to meditate or just be at one with nature. This visualization
knotting spell will lead you back to the center of yourself,
so your spiritual side gets a say in your daily life too.

In ancient Mesopotamian mythology, the garden of the gods was a place where the Sumerian hero, Utnapishtim, was given eternal life. Near the source of a great river, beneath a mountain range, this garden was magical—a paradise of trees bearing gemstones, crystals, and pearls from the sea.

Similarly, you are going to walk through the garden of the gods and be at the source of all that is, to awaken and nurture your spiritual self.

Find a quiet place, light a white candle to invoke spiritual energy around you, and close your eyes.

Imagine you are walking through a dense wood; you reach a clearing, cross a stream, and look up to high mountains covered in cedars and a waterfall tumbling down into a deep river. There you stop to take

a drink of water, and notice a strange, but beautiful, garden. Every tree is a tangle of lush branches bearing extraordinary fruits of gemstones, lapis lazuli, carnelian, agate, and huge pearls.

On one bush climbs a vine dazzling with nine huge pearls. You pick the pearls and place them on the ground. In this garden you laze under the Sun until it sets. When the Full Moon appears in the sky, you pluck one of the moonbeam threads from above and start to knot your pearls to make a string of pearls. When you finish threading the pearls, you kiss each of them and give thanks to the Garden of the Gods. You carry on your way, leaving the necklace behind as a gift to the garden. You know you can return there whenever you like and take up your pearl necklace to bring you enlightenment and spiritual healing.

WHEN TO CAST SPELL

First
Quarter
Moon

Universal Truth Spell

This spell asks you to affirm what matters most to you in life,
whether it's to be creative, belong to something or someone,
or have a great vocation. What matters to us most gives us
a deep, unequivocal connection to the Universe.

Being true to your deepest
self is a connection to
the inner you, the place
where you and the Universe merge,
and that's a feeling we often get
when we are apparently consumed
by creativity, love, or a passion for
something. Yet deep down inside we
know this really matters to us. So,
whatever it is that matters to you,
it's time to knot it into your life and
connect to your own universal truth.
Before you begin, focus on what
matters to you most. Pose yourself
some questions. Ask yourself in the
mirror what it is that makes you feel
a deep sense of self and what makes
you feel profound joy. If you don't
know yet, then don't perform the
spell until you do, as it's very hard to
untie this particular knot!

WHAT YOU WILL NEED

3 x 2ft (60cm) white ribbons

Indelible pen

SPELL CASTING

When you know what matters to
you, write it down on each of the
ribbons. Then, take your ribbons
and go out into the countryside or
a place which is not too public—
anywhere in nature to reinforce
your connection to the Universe.

Stand on your chosen spot and
make a knot in the middle of each
of your ribbons, then knot the
three together to make a triangular
shape. As you do so, say the charm
(opposite).

Place the knotted triangle on the
ground and step into the middle,
then raise your face and arms to the
sky and say:

*"Bless the Universe for the
truth of me."*

When you step out of the triangle,
take your ribbons with you, and
whatever truly matters to you will
begin to work itself into your life
and bring you that joyful connection
to the Universe you are looking for.

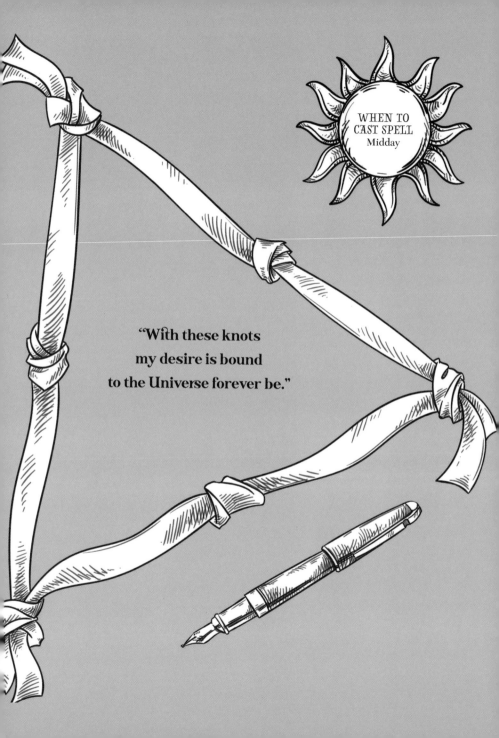

"With these knots
my desire is bound
to the Universe forever be."

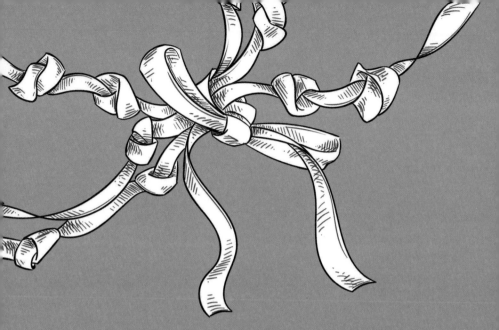

CHAPTER SIX

Travel & Adventure

SPELLS

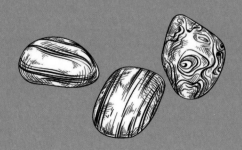

Are you on your travels or about to start a new
adventure? These spells will ensure not only
safe voyages, but also enhance your potential
for success and enjoyment anywhere you go.
With charms to protect you en route and luck
for gambles and risks, as well as an enchantment
to decide where to set off next, you will be
able to make a positive move forward to any
destination. If you're simply looking for courage
to start a new venture, then a visualization
spell will enhance your true brave spirit.

A Charm for Successful Traveling

You may be about to travel the world, or just take a trip to another part of it, but wherever you're going, this charm will ensure you have a successful, happy time away from home.

Many of us long for adventure, the lure of the open road, and a need to break free from the ties that often bind us to routines or keep us stuck in a rut. We may resent being beholden to work, money, and family, but fear the outcome if we were to take time out. Whether you feel this craving for escape or just a dose of much-needed freedom from it all, like many ancient travelers, all it needs is the magic of the empowering energy of the World Tarot card to light the way. This card symbolizes your ability to go out and travel without fear or worry, and, with a knotted sunstone beside you in a pouch, you will be blessed with happy travels.

WHAT YOU WILL NEED

The World tarot card (as drawn opposite)

Sunstone

1ft (30cm) length of gold-colored cord

Small silk pouch (or purse)

SPELL CASTING

Open the book on this page and use the World Tarot card image opposite. Place the sunstone in the center of the card and repeat the enchantment (opposite).

Next, take up the length of cord and make a binding Surgeon's Knot (see page 124). This is a stronger version of a Reef Knot and represents harmony between your adventurous self and the pathway you are about to take. Place the knotted cord on the Tarot card and repeat the spell.

Finally, take the knotted cord and sunstone and place them in the pouch. Keep this with you throughout your travels and you will be rewarded with beneficial energy and a golden journey filled with joy and laughter.

"The World will see me joys untold
This stone to bring me journeys bold.
The power of gold a route to follow
This binding knot for all tomorrows.
With this charm I will be refreshed
And all my travels be truly blessed."

WHEN TO
CAST SPELL
The day before
you set off on
your travels

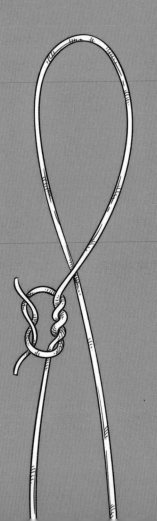

THE WORLD

Spell to Express the Adventurer in You

There are times when we have a niggling desire to step outside our comfort zone. We yearn to do something different, challenging, or even madcap. This spell will enable you to free up that debonair side of yourself ready for any new experience.

Adventure isn't just about traveling, although it can be. It's also about taking a step forward into an unknown territory that may be creative, physically or mentally challenging, spiritually enlightening, or simply starting afresh in a new location. Whatever adventure you are hoping for, this spell will offer protection and good vibes. Hermes was the Greek god of travelers and his winged sandals enabled him to fly between Earth and the heavens. As a guide of transitions, he will enable you to embrace that mercurial spirit within yourself and cross any threshold out of your comfort zone and into an unknown one.

WHAT YOU WILL NEED

Envelope

Pen

4 short yellow ribbons

SPELL CASTING

Take the envelope and write down on the outside what kind of adventure you are about to experience. To make Hermes' good luck charm, tie Multiple Overhand Knots (see page 122) in three of the yellow ribbons, then bind the three together with the fourth ribbon using a Reef Knot (see page 121). Then say the charm (opposite). The overhand knot is renowned for its strength and resilience to being untied.

Now place your good luck charm in the envelope to affirm your intention to the god himself.

Seal the envelope and take it with you on your new venture to enhance all self-belief, confidence, and your own enveloped spirit bound on your quest.

"With three and four I make thus seven
The path to all that brings me heaven.
Out of my comfort zone now I fly
With Hermes' help to reach the sky.
Boundless and fearless I cross the line
To make a charm for my design."

WHEN TO
CAST SPELL
A New Crescent
Moon or just
before embarking
on a new venture

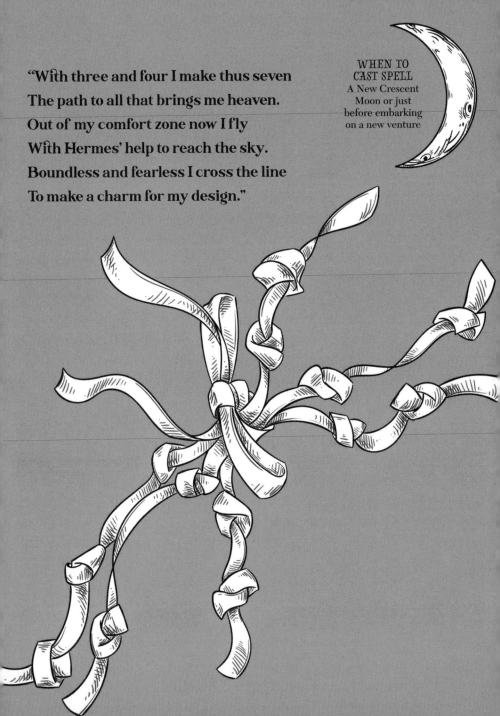

Talisman to Protect from Negative Influences when Traveling

Whether you're going by foot, bike, plane, car, or train, negative electromagnetic energy and geopathic stress is everywhere. This charm will protect you wherever you go.

Negative energy obviously changes as you pass through a variety of different environments, so carrying this talisman will protect you from all of it. For example, in the airport you're going to be exposed to security scanners and X-ray machines. As you track across unknown territory, what lies above and beneath you? Electricity pylons, underground water courses, negative ley lines, or even burial grounds? In most ancient traditions, travelers wouldn't venture forth without taking some form of protective talisman. Chinese traders carried amulets made from crystals such as jade, malachite, and shungite. They even knotted them into the sleeves of their robes to protect them from robbers.

WHAT YOU WILL NEED

3ft (90cm) length of green or black cord

3 pieces of shungite or malachite

White candle

Lighter or matches

SPELL CASTING

Make a Monkey Braid (see page 118) with the cord, but don't tie off the ends. As you loop the knots, say the names of the places you intend to visit. If you're off to destinations unknown, just say, "destinations unknown." Lay the braid on a table horizontally in front of you. Take the three crystals and place them in a triangle above the braid.

Place the lit candle in the center of the triangle and repeat the spell (opposite). Then, take up the braid and pull the ends so that all the knots disappear, and all future negative energy with them. Wind the cord round the triangle of crystals to seal your intention.

Let the candle burn down for 10 minutes to amplify your request for protection, then blow it out. Take up the cord and choose one crystal to take with you in your pocket to create a powerful shield of protection. Leave the other two crystals and the cord in a safe place.

WHEN TO
CAST SPELL
The evening before
you travel

"Wherever I go I will be safe
with this talisman's power
to shield me from all."

Labyrinth Knot-seeing Spell for Courage

Sometimes we need a spot of courage before we venture into the unknown. This easy meditation will bring you the boldness you seek.

In Greek mythology, Ariadne, the daughter of the Cretan King Minos, gave Theseus a ball of thread so that he could find his way out of the labyrinth after his quest to destroy the Minotaur. This knot-seeing visualization will see you get through the labyrinth to confront your own fears, represented by the Minotaur, and then return to the light of day to show you have daring and the spark of adventure.

On the opposite page is a labyrinth. In the chamber at the center is the embodiment of your fearless self, the Minotaur, half-man, half-bull, tied to a boulder. On the outside of the labyrinth is a ball of golden thread.

Find somewhere quiet, close your eyes, and relax for a few minutes. Focus on your adventure or why you need to rediscover your brave spirit or questing nature. Now open your eyes and gaze into the labyrinth.

Imagine you pick up the ball of thread and set off down the first tunnel. You don't know which tunnel to go down, but you are determined to reach the center, free the bull, and then return to the light again. This is a very dark place; there are empty rooms, shadows around every corner, and, as you venture deeper into the maze, you feel apprehensive, but certain that you will find the bull's chamber. As you walk through the tunnels you let the golden thread unravel behind you. As you turn a corner, the bull turns to greet you. He is strong, but gentle, fierce but accepting, sure of himself, but willing to share his power. You unknot the chain that binds him to the rock and let it fall to the ground. You ask him if he will go with you, but he shakes his head. He is free to go when he pleases, but blesses you to adventure forth now. You thank him and then take up the ball of thread and wind it back into a ball as you follow your pathway back to the light. With the blessing of the Minotaur you feel uplifted and sure of your direction. As you reach daylight, you take the golden ball of thread and place it in your backpack, ready for anything.

Come out of your visualization, and you will now have freed up your fearless side.

WHEN TO
CAST SPELL
First Quarter
Moon

Good Luck Charm for Gambles, Risks, and Challenges

We all want to take a gamble or risk at times. This simple, but effective, knot spell will bring you luck in whatever venture you undertake or challenge you aspire to.

Feng shui is about creating harmony in the home by the placement of objects and symbols. When balanced, the five elements of Chinese astrology promote the perfect environment for happiness. But, according to ancient tradition, when the elements are symbolically carried as knotted silk scarves, tied into robes or attached to headwear or weaponry, they also bring the wearer luck in all forms of gambling or risk-taking. The five elements are Fire, Earth, Water, Metal, and Wood, and each corresponds to various compass directions: Fire to the South, Water to the North, Wood to the East, Metal to the West, and Earth to the Southwest.

WHAT YOU WILL NEED

5 small square silk scarves in the following colors:

Red
Blue
Green
White
Yellow

Gold thread

SPELL CASTING

Take the scarves one by one, fold them diagonally, and make a big double knot in the center. Place the red scarf in the South part of your home (to boost Fire energy); the blue scarf in the North part of your home (to boost Water energy); the yellow scarf in the East corner (to boost Wood energy); the green in the Southwest (to boost Earth enery); and the white in the West (to boost Metal energy).

Leave the scarves for 24 hours, then gather them together the next day, tie them up in a length of golden thread, and take them with you in your bag or in your pocket when you want to go gambling, take a risk, or start a new challenge.

WHEN TO
CAST SPELL
A full 24 hours
before you
take a risk

N

W

E

SW

S

Spell so you Don't Get Lost on Your Travels

Now that you are confident enough to set off into the unknown, it's a good idea to have the blessing of a spiritual deity to keep you from getting lost and to keep you on track for your purpose.

In Roman mythology, Janus was the god of transitions and new beginnings. Depicted with one head facing the future and one looking to the past, he was also the god of time, beginnings, and doorways. He was petitioned when setting off with a purpose, a goal, and a reason to travel somewhere. Roman travelers would invoke his help by wearing a knotted belt with golden rings and a lock of their hair so they wouldn't get lost. With the help of Janus, this knotting spell will ensure you don't stray off your chosen pathway and will keep you safe and set on your destination.

WHAT YOU WILL NEED

Gold ring

Lock of your own hair

A very long white cord (long enough to tie 21 knots and then tie round your waist)

Citrus oil

White candle

Lighter and matches

Small silk pouch (or purse)

SPELL CASTING

Anoint and bless the ring, lock of hair, and cord by drizzling citrus oil across the ingredients. Light the candle and begin to make 21 knots (any knot you prefer) in close groups of three, along the length of the white cord. As you do this, repeat the enchantment (opposite).

Take up the lock of hair and the ring, and place them in the pouch. Wind the knotted cord around your waist and tie it into a bow. To bind the spell to you, bring Janus' blessing, and keep you on the right pathway, repeat the spell, then take off the belt and put it in your suitcase with the pouch.

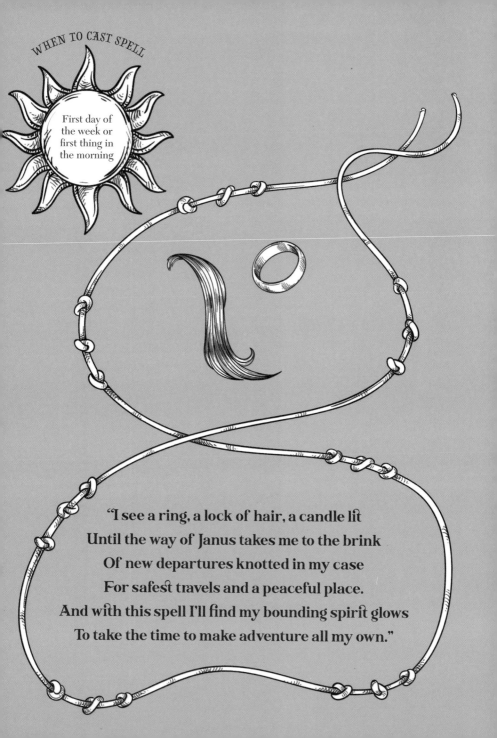

First day of
the week or
first thing in
the morning

"I see a ring, a lock of hair, a candle lit
Until the way of Janus takes me to the brink
Of new departures knotted in my case
For safest travels and a peaceful place.
And with this spell I'll find my bounding spirit glows
To take the time to make adventure all my own."

Where to Go Next
Divination Spell

You may have already had quite a few adventures or exciting experiences, so where to now? Can you have something even more breathtaking, more unforgettable? This spell will help you know where and how.

On the opposite page is a magic circle made up of animal spirit guide footprints—places where the spirits have passed by and left traces of their energy in our lives, often without us knowing. These are your animal guides and, as you unravel each knot to represent the seven spirits, you will discover which advice you need to follow.

WHAT YOU WILL NEED

7 x 1ft (30cm) lengths of fine red thread

Magic Circle (as drawn opposite)

SPELL CASTING

Take up the seven red threads and tie each in the center with any knot.

As each guide is associated with a different quality and quest, place a knot on each of the animal footprints and say:

"Where next to go, all set for traveling? This knot will tell by its unraveling."

Focus on the Magic Circle for a few minutes, then, starting in the East and moving in a clockwise direction, pick up and unravel each knot. Focus on the animal's attributes. The easier it is to unravel the knot, the more likely this is your true way forward. If you feel an affinity to any of the guides, this can also suggest they are connecting deeply with you. Follow the path in the way suggested by your guide.

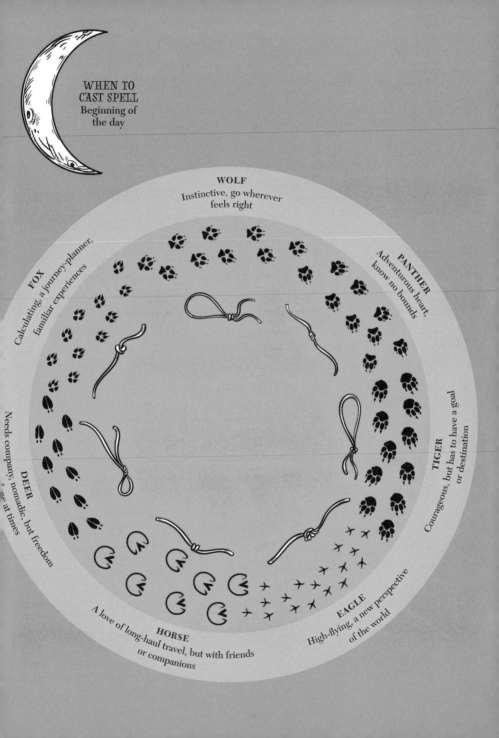

WHEN TO
CAST SPELL
Beginning of
the day

WOLF
Instinctive, go wherever
feels right

FOX
Calculating, a journey-planner,
familiar experiences

PANTHER
Adventurous heart,
know no bounds

TIGER
Courageous, but has to have a goal
or destination

DEER
Needs company; nomadic, but freedom
... me at times

EAGLE
High-flying, a new perspective
of the world

HORSE
A love of long-haul travel, but with friends
or companions

CHAPTER SEVEN

Knot

DIRECTORY

This section shows you how to make more complicated knots that are specific to certain spells. If you find it hard to follow the instructions, you can still use any old knot if you so desire. These knots will, however, reinforce the meaning, intention, and result of your spell because they are powerful symbolic elements linked to the specific charm. Whether you want to seal a deal that is unbreakable or to break free from a short-lived spell, this section will give you the added ingredient to make that magic work for you.

Monkey Braid

The Monkey Braid transforms one piece of string into a pretty braid, and, as a magical device, manifests as many rewards as we make knots from just one spell.

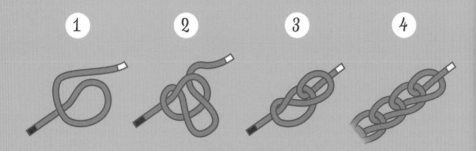

1	2	3	4
Loop the right-hand end of the cord over itself, near to the left-hand end of the cord to form a loop.	Take the right-hand side of the cord and push it through the loop to create a second loop. Pull this second loop down, through the first loop and out, tugging it toward the working side of the cord to tighten it slightly.	Once you have pulled the U-shaped second loop through the first loop, pull it to the right-hand side so that it is in line with the braid and the loop that you just pulled it through.	Repeat steps 2 and 3 as necessary down the length of the cord to create new loops and complete the braid. To finish the braid, pass the right-hand end of the cord through the last loop. Pull firmly on both loose ends of the cord to tighten the braid.

Celtic Knot

The Celtic knot is a traditional symbol representing infinity and the power of eternal love. Use it in friendship and love spells to create an unbreakable bond.

1

2

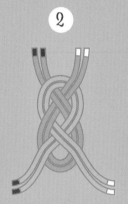

3

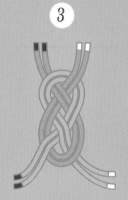

Line up two pieces of cord, and fold them in half to form a loop. With the loop facing you, overlap the right end over the left.

Line up another two lengths of cord and begin weaving them through the crossover loop you created. From the left, pass over the loop itself and then under the right tail end, just behind the overlap point. Next, pass the cords over the left tail end and then underneath the loop on the left side. Come up through the loop and over the tail ends of the cords you are currently weaving.

Pass the cords back underneath the loop again on the right side. Adjust the cord as needed, gently guiding the cords through the woven knot so that all eight tail ends are even and the cords are not twisted inside the knot, then pull the knot tight.

Figure Eight Braid

The Figure Eight Braid is a knot that brings strength
and purpose to a spell, reinforcing your goals and
enhancing your connection to the Universe.

1

2

Line up the two pieces
of cord with the working
ends facing in opposite
directions. Pass the working
end of the cord down and
around the standing part
and back up through
the loop.

Tighten by working the knot
together so that both knots
lie neat and snug together.

Reef Knot

Reef Knots are often used in traditional magic to represent harmony, equality, balance, and togetherness, but they must be tied exactly as shown.

Take the right working end of the cord over and under the left to create a loop. Bring the left working end over and under the right.

Tuck and pull firmly to secure.

Multiple Overhand Knots

A knot that's always difficult to untie, and used in magic spells, the Overhand Knot enhances strength, resilience, and the powerful determination to succeed.

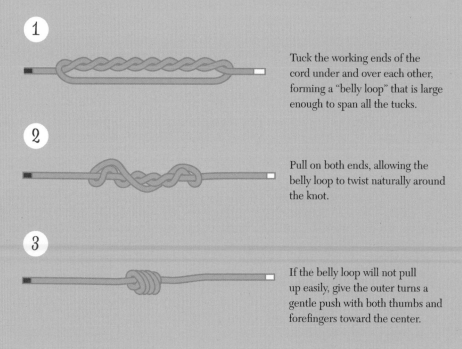

1

Tuck the working ends of the cord under and over each other, forming a "belly loop" that is large enough to span all the tucks.

2

Pull on both ends, allowing the belly loop to twist naturally around the knot.

3

If the belly loop will not pull up easily, give the outer turns a gentle push with both thumbs and forefingers toward the center.

Four-strand Flat Plait

A Four-strand Plait doubles the intention behind the spell
and creates peaceful, empowering energy as you weave. If
you can do a three-strand braid, four is easy to master.

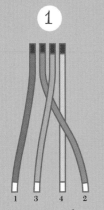
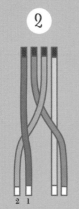

1 Line up your four lengths of cord. Start by taking cord two under cord three and over four.

2 Renumber your cords 1–4 from left to right. Then take cord one over cord two.

3 Take the two center cords and pass the right-hand cord over the left.

4 Now repeat this pattern: Outer left cord over second cord and into the middle; outer right cord under third cord and over the second cord.

Surgeon's Knot

Known for its incredible holding power, in traditional magic, this knot is
used to secure magic pouches or complete spells with longevity in mind.

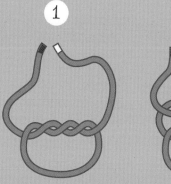

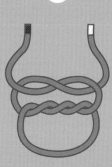

Take the right working end
of the cord over and under
the left to create a loop.
Repeat this once more.

Take the right cord over and
under the left cord, and pull
to secure.

Blood Knot

Almost impossible to untie, this knot is used in magic to seal a deal or ensure the protection, importance, and empowerment of family ties.

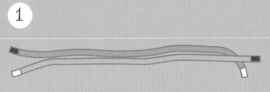

1

Lay the two cords parallel with the working ends facing in opposite directions.

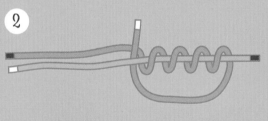

2

With one cord, make four turns around the standing second cord. Bring the working end back to the start of the turns and pass it between its own standing part and the second cord.

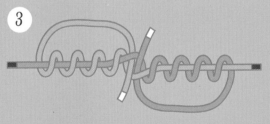

3

Take the working end of the second cord and make the same number of turns around the standing part of the first cord, feeding the working end back into the center of the knot, but in the opposite direction to the first. Pull the cords to tighten.

Index

REMEMBER THE WITCHES' OATH:

"I will only do
what I do
for the good of all."

By knot of one, the spell's begun

By knot of two, it cometh true

By knot of three, so mote it be

By knot of four, this power I store

By knot of five, the spell's alive

By knot of six, this spell I fix

By knot of seven, events I'll leaven

By knot of eight, it will be fate

By knot of nine, what's done is mine